DISCOVER
UNEXPECTED
LONDON

DISCOVER
UNEXPECTED
LONDON

ANDREW LAWSON

PHAIDON

To the memory of my father
William Halford Lawson KBE, (1899–1971)

Acknowledgements

Grateful thanks to many individuals who have helped me in my work on this book. My friend, Bill Evans has let me use three of his photographs (**64, 163, 218**). The Public Records Office, Chancery Lane, gave permission to reproduce the swan-marks manuscript in their Museum (**231**). Dr Igor Anrep allowed me to photograph the mosaic by his father on the floor of the National Gallery (**4**).

The following were kind enough to permit me to take photographs of events on private premises: The Under Treasurer of the Honourable Society of the Middle Temple (**67**); The Clerk of the Worshipful Company of Goldsmiths (**35**): Master Jacob, the Queen's Remembrancer (**46**): Mr Broughton, Verger of the Church of St Andrew Undershaft (**47**): The Headmaster of Westminster School (**54**): The Reverend Mother of St Ethelreda's Convent School, Ely Place (**63**). Warm thanks to the ladies and gentlemen who let me photograph them at work (The Tradesmen) and standing to attention in their uniforms (London Dress).

I should like to acknowledge the encouragement and support that I have received from Professor Trevor-Roper, Drs A. A. M. van der Heyden, and Herman Friedhoff.

Design: Richard Brooks/Keith Russell

Phaidon Press Ltd., Littlegate House, St Ebbe's Street, Oxford

First published 1977 by Elsevier-Phaidon. Second edition (paperback) 1979

ISBN 0 7148 2019 9

Planned and produced by Elsevier International Projects Ltd, Oxford
© 1977 Elsevier Publishing Projects SA, Lausanne

Filmset by Keyspools Ltd, Golborne, Lancashire
Printed by Jolly & Barber Ltd, Rugby, England

Title page: 1 An election day procession. When the Vintners' Company process to church after the election of their new Master, they are led by one of their wine porters, in smock and top hat, who sweeps the road clear with a birch broom. The custom dates from the days when horse transport made the streets of London as hazardous as a farmyard for a well-shod gentleman. Nosegays helped to mask the stench.

Contents

2 A sewer gas lamp.
Guests at the Savoy,
one of London's top
hotels, are usually
unaware of the discreet
hygiene of this street
lamp nearby. Dating
from around 1900, the
lamp burns up the
noxious gases from the
Savoy sewers below.
This one is the last of
its kind in London.
*Carting Lane, Strand,
WC2*

Introduction

This is a book about London: its ancient survivals, living traditions, hidden beauties, forgotten memorials of men and events, arcane and entrancing histories, curious juxtapositions.

London, like any historic metropolis, is multiform, multidimensional. It has been for centuries a port, a capital, a mercantile city; and because it is English, and therefore both anarchical and continuous, it has absorbed and preserved the deposit of all those centuries. And yet behind all these enjoyable archaisms is a continuing vitality which proves that they are not mere archaisms. The monarchy with its formal pageantry, the City with its antique privileges, the Law-courts with their ritual, the Tower with its grim memories, everything is gradually changed but nothing is ever ended. The monarch still rides in state to open Parliament, the Lord Mayor still puts on his show, the inns of court retain their collegiate structure, the Tower may still hold prisoners of state. And what is true of these great structures and formal occasions is true also of its humbler citizens and their more private traditions. There is a tribalism of hatters and boot-makers, a subculture of milkmen and fish-porters, a sophistication and hierarchy of costermongers.

The great capitals of Continental Europe bear the marks of authority. Henri IV and Napoleon left their mark on Paris. Rome is the city of the renaissance Popes. Lisbon, levelled by the earthquake in 1755, is the Lisbon of Pombal. But London has consistently resisted well-meaning authority. It defied the political symmetry of Stuart kings and the architectural symmetry of great artists. The renaissance did not touch it. Its medieval "liberties" and "peculiars" defied the modernity of the Tudors. We had no "benevolent despots" in the eighteenth century, no strategic boulevards in the nineteenth. Periodically, there have been attempts at "urbanism." Sir Christopher Wren would have reorganized the City after the Great Fire. When the defeat of Napoleon was in sight, Nash planned a magnificent Regency capital. During the last war, when the defeat of Hitler could similarly be foreseen, plans were drawn up for a new London. The Great Blitz, like the Great Fire, offered an opportunity to the ambitious architects of triumphal arches and majestic malls. But the Londoners atomised all these splendid projects in turn. London is still, in spite of all its developers, a congeries of villages, a city of people.

Not being a Londoner, I discover London, as it was built, discontinuously and piecemeal; and being a historian I tend to discover it historically. How much the names tell a historian! Foreigners change their street-names with each revolution. We keep ours; and being kept, they tell us their history. The names in the Strand are Jacobean, with a surviving substructure of the medieval Church – of the bishops' "inns" along the river. Along Piccadilly we recognize the frivolous courtiers of Charles II – Jermyn, Babmaes, Arlington, Clifford. Northwards and westwards, formal streets and squares advertise the great aristocratic developers of the seventeenth and eighteenth centuries – Russells and Harleys, Bentincks and Cavendishes.

These developers have imposed their names; but behind the names are other names, a palimpsest of dateable symbols, and behind them, in turn, always breaking through, are the living realities which absolutely refuse to be absorbed. It is these realities which animate this book and make it a unique record of London life.

In the past, the great danger to the variety of London life and its monuments has been "development." It was the ruthless "development" of the sixteenth century – the destruction of churches and church property, the defacement of images and tombs, and crosses and stained glass – which caused the first great chronicler of London, the tailor John Stow, to write his famous *Survey*. In our own time "conservationists" struggle weakly against the bulldozer and the impersonal office block. But perhaps a greater threat than the physical destruction of buildings is the economic destruction of that human variety and sophistication of which architectural variety is the expression. The mass age, with its economic and social uniformity, is the last and most deadly enemy of cultural vitality.

"A ceremony or ritual remains convincing," says Mr. Lawson, "so long as its participants understand its history and are certain of its value. As soon as an event is re-enacted solely as a public spectacle it becomes, at best, theatre and, at worst, pantomime." The London which is here portrayed is not yet, happily, either theatre or pantomime. What Mr. Lawson has captured is a living spirit, the expression of a genuine, continuous urban life.

This is an enchanting book. It will delight anyone who knows, or wants to know, London.

Hugh Trevor-Roper

3 A Charity Boy. This figure and its female counterpart were used to mark a school run by charity. This one dates from 1821 (see pages 46–7). *St Botolph's Church Hall, Bishopsgate, EC2*

Regius Professor of Modern History, University of Oxford

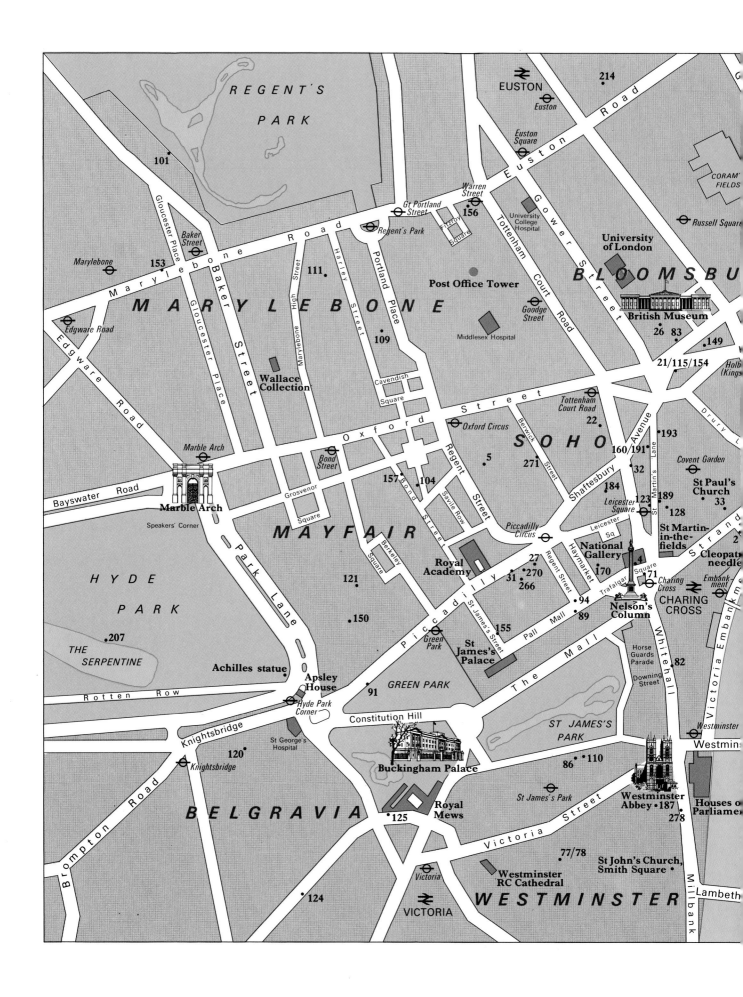

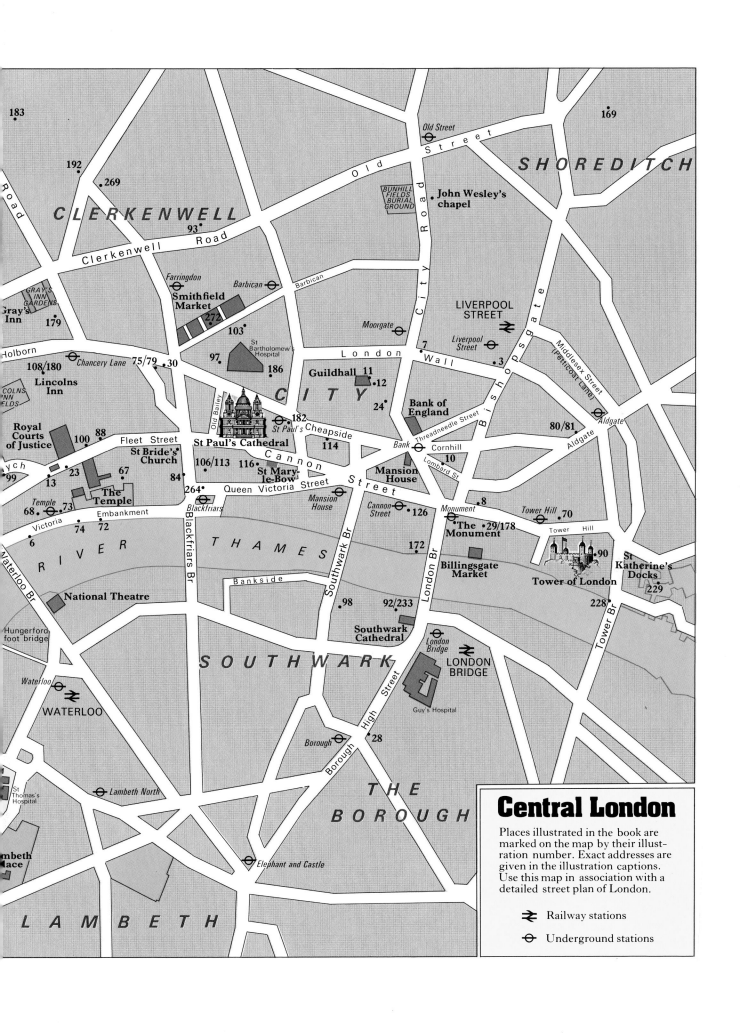

183

169

Old Street

SHOREDITCH

Old Street

City   Road

BUNHILL
FIELDS
BURIAL
GROUND

**John Wesley's
chapel**

192

269

CLERKENWELL

93

Clerkenwell   Road

Farringdon

Barbican

Barbican

**LIVERPOOL
STREET**

**Smithfield
Market**

272

Moorgate

Liverpool
Street

**LIVERPOOL
STREET**

Middlesex Street
(Petticoat Lane)

GRAY'S
INN
GARDENS

103

St
Bartholomew's
Hospital

London   Wall

7

3

GRAY'S
INN

Gray's
Inn

179

Holborn

108/180

Chancery Lane

75/79 30

97

186

Guildhall 11

12

80/81

Aldgate

LINCOLNS
INN
FIELDS

**Lincolns
Inn**

CITY

24

**Bank of
England**

Aldgate

182

St Paul's Cheapside

Threadneedle Street

**Royal
Courts
of Justice**

100 88

Old Bailey

Bishopsgate

ych

99

Fleet   Street

St Paul's Cathedral

114

Bank

Cornhill

10

80/81

**St Bride's
Church**

106/113 116

**St Mary-
le-Bow**

Cannon

Lombard St

8

13 23

67

84

Mansion
House

**Mansion
House**

Tower Hill

70

68

Temple

73

**The
Temple**

264

Queen Victoria Street

Street

Cannon
Street

126

Monument

Tower   Hill

74 72

Victoria

Embankment

Blackfriars

Mansion
House

172

The •29/178
Monument

90

6

RIVER

Blackfriars Br

THAMES

London Br

8

St
Katherine's
Docks

Tower of London

229

Southwark Br

Bankside

**Billingsgate
Market**

228

Tower Br

National Theatre

98

92/233

London
Bridge

LONDON
BRIDGE

Hungerford
foot bridge

**Southwark
Cathedral**

SOUTHWARK

Waterloo

High   Street

WATERLOO

Guy's Hospital

St
Thomas's
Hospital

Lambeth North

Borough

28

Borough

*THE
BOROUGH*

mbeth
ace

Elephant and Castle

LAMBETH

Central London

Places illustrated in the book are
marked on the map by their illustration number. Exact addresses are
given in the illustration captions.
Use this map in association with a
detailed street plan of London.

⇌ Railway stations

⊖ Underground stations

A chronology of London

55–54 BC	Roman invasion of Britain. No mention of London in Julius Caesar's account.
43 AD	The Romans, under Claudius, occupy Britain. London becomes a major trading centre. First London Bridge built of wood.
61	Revolt of the Iceni, under Queen Boudicea. London burnt.
c 200	The Romans build London Wall, 2 miles long, 20 feet high.
410	Roman occupation ends.
604	St Augustine consecrates Mellitus as Bishop of London. Building begins of first St Paul's Cathedral.
616	Legendary consecration of first Abbey at Westminster.
787–	Frequent attacks on London by Danes.
1014	Olaf the Norseman brings down London Bridge by attaching ropes to the timbers and rowing hard downstream ("London Bridge is falling down").
1065	Consecration of Edward the Confessor's Westminster Abbey.
1066	William the Conqueror crowned in Westminster Abbey.
1081–97	The White Tower at the Tower of London built.
1176–	London Bridge built in stone.
1209	(It survived until 1831.)
1292	Lincoln's Inn, first of the Inns of Court, founded.
c 1300	Trade guilds receive first royal charters from Edward I.
1348–9	The Black Death. 10,000 Londoners die.
1381	The Peasants' Revolt. Mayor Walworth slays the rebel leader, Wat Tyler, at Smithfield.
1476	William Caxton sets up his printing press at Westminster.
1528–39	Dissolution of the monasteries and confiscation of their lands, begun by suppressing Holy Trinity, Aldgate.
1531	Henry VIII takes over St James's leper hospital and builds a palace there. Hyde Park becomes his hunting forest.
1537	Henry VIII founds the Honourable Artillery Company, the City of London's own regiment.
1576	Opening of the Theatre, London's first playhouse, by James Burbage.
1605	The Gunpowder Plot. Guy Fawkes tries to blow up Parliament and the king.
1632	Inigo Jones lays out London's first square, in Covent Garden.
1642	Charles I tries to impeach five members of Parliament. The Civil War begins between Royalists and Parliamentarians. London goes against the king.
1649	Charles I tried in Westminster Hall and executed in Whitehall.
1649–60	Commonwealth Government. The puritans ban entertainments and festivities, including church singing and Christmas celebrations.
1652	London's first coffee house opened in St Michael's Alley, Cornhill.
1660	Restoration of the monarchy. Charles II enters London in triumph (May 29th).
1663	First Theatre Royal, Drury Lane opened.
1665	Russian ambassador presents king with pelicans for St James's. The Plague. 100,000 Londoners die.
1666	The Great Fire. St Paul's Cathedral, 88 other churches and 13,200 homes – four-fifths of the City – devastated.
1675–1711	Sir Christopher Wren superintends the building of the new St Paul's.
1685	Huguenot refugees settle in London, chiefly in Spitalfields.
1694	Bank of England established in the City.
1698	Whitehall Palace burns. The Court moves to St James's.
1703	Buckingham House built. Remodelled by John Nash in 1829 it did not become the royal palace until 1837 when Victoria moved in.
1739–49	Westminster Bridge built.
1759	The British Museum opened in Montague House.
1768	The Royal Academy established.
1801	First accurate census: population 864,000.
1800–05	London Docks built.
1802	Madame Tussaud opens her first waxworks in the Strand.
1826	University College founded. London Zoological Society founded.
1829	The Metropolitan Police founded by Sir Robert Peel.
1831	New London Bridge built. (Exported to Arizona when replaced in 1968–72.)
1834	The Palace of Westminster destroyed by fire. Turner paints the scene.
1836	London's first railway station opened at London Bridge.
1839–60	The new Palace of Westminster built by Barry and Pugin.
1851	Prince Albert organizes the Great Exhibition in Hyde Park. Paxton's glass hall was later moved to Crystal Palace.
1863	First underground railway between Farringdon and Paddington.
1864–70	Joseph Bazalgette constructs the Thames Embankment.
1868	Last public execution in London.
1872	Albert Hall opened.
1881	Population reaches 3,330,000.
1888	London County Council set up, but the Lord Mayor retains power over the City which remains independent.
1914–18	The First World War. 25 air raids on London; 1,000 civilians killed.
1939–45	The Second World War. Autumn 1940, the blitz on London begins. A third of the City devastated; 30,000 civilians killed.
1951	The Festival of Britain. The South Bank becomes an arts centre.
1952	Agatha Christie's "The Mousetrap" opens at the Ambassadors Theatre.
1953	Coronation of Her Majesty Queen Elizabeth II at Westminster Abbey on June 2nd.
1963	Beginning of the Barbican development to bring 6,500 new residents into the depopulated City of London.
1964	The Post Office Tower built, 619 feet high.
1965	Creation of the Greater London Council.
1971	Population 7,379,000, but falling.
1976	National Theatre opened.

A London viewpoint

Gladstone said that the best way to see London was from the top of an omnibus. In his day, buses were open to the air and the passengers' heads would be brushed by the branches of passing trees. Signs could be studied in close detail and the smells of the London streets enjoyed at a comfortable distance.

Today it is still a pleasure to travel across London on the top of a bus, although now one is insulated from the world outside like an apple under cellophane. A good way to enjoy the bus is to buy a Red Rover ticket which gives free access to any red bus for a period. One can take one's chance, swinging across London along unknown routes, without plan or purpose, sometimes ending up at unheard-of termini. If one is bored it is easy to get off, cross the road and catch the next bus going in the opposite direction.

But the best way to see the city is to go on foot. London is a shy old lady, discreet, reserved and unostentatious about her charms. She does not reveal much to the man in a hurry or to the tourist who is most intent upon ticking off his list of official, or even unexpected, sights. London speaks to the dawdler, to the wanderer up side streets; here are to be found some of the keyholes into London's past. London's history is written on her walls and carved on her buildings. There are even snatches of history in the idioms of everyday London speech.

History is celebrated in custom and ritual. Monarchs and leaders of long ago are remembered affectionately like private friends. The drummer of the Grenadier Guards wears a black armband in mourning for Charles II and the Pensioners of the Royal Hospital, Chelsea, raise their hats for the same king as if he were an old comrade. The city also remembers her more humble citizens, such as the inventor, in 1857, of an elastic glue, or the hero who died under the approaching train from Kew while rescuing a workman on the line.

London is full of surprises. The last place that one would expect to find a portrait of Greta Garbo is in the National Gallery in London. Indeed most people pass by without noticing her. In fact they very often tread on her, for her face appears in the mosaic in the entrance hall, across which art-lovers hurriedly pass on their way to enjoy the Rembrandts and the Cézannes. Garbo's portrait is labelled "Melpomena" and she represents the Muse of Tragedy. In another panel, the artist Augustus John poses as Neptune. T. S. Eliot, the poet, depicts leisure and he is shown in an uncomfort-

able pose, contemplating at once the Loch Ness Monster and Einstein's formula, $E = mc^2$. As Lucidity, Bertrand Russell is shown pulling Truth from a well and stripping off her mask. Among themes that represent the pleasures of life are the most unassuming Still Lives that one could ever hope to see in a national art gallery – a picture of a humble Christmas pudding, and beside it, a mud pie.

The spirit of the people of London is quirky and idiosyncratic and coloured with wit and with human warmth. It is a spirit that has survived the Roman occupation, Norse invasions, William's conquering, the Black Death, the Plague, the Great Fire, the Blitz, the Redevelopment of the 1960's, and which will ride the present economic discomfort as if it were nothing worse than a few bones in a plate of eels.

4 Greta Garbo; mosaic by Boris Anrep (1933), on the floor of the National Gallery entrance lobby.
National Gallery, Trafalgar Sq. SW1

Looking up in London

nan children's book
te for "Little Johnny
where he was going.
shes laughed at him.
idon would soon step
y a bus. But before he
n some strange and

y and the craftsman's
ed and printed on
i of vandals, antique
ilike. Indeed, some of
idon buildings are so
y seem to have been
ment of steeplejacks

ited the great Gothic
churches of England must have worked for their own
satisfaction or to please the angels, because some of
their exquisite detailing is quite invisible from ground
level. In many Neo-Gothic buildings of the nineteenth
century the carvers were of the same mould, working
evidently for their own amusement. The grotesques on
St Giles' Church, Camberwell, now sadly eroded by
the weather, were carved as caricatures of politicians of
the day. Gladstone is up there and so too are Lord
Randolph Churchill, William Wilberforce and Lord
Salisbury. As they are now in need of renewal it would
be in keeping if these heads were replaced by those of
our own contemporary politicians. This might at least
ensure that they are not forgotten by posterity.

Perched high above Cornhill in the City, silhouetted
against the sky, are a pair of crouching devils that seem
poised to leap down on to the Church of St Peter below
them. There is a story attached to these unlikable
decorations. In planning his designs for the building of
55 Cornhill the architect, named Runtz, had a dispute
with the authorities of the Wren church next door. He
lost, but he got his own back on them by calling up
these devils to express his disfavour long after he was
dead.

5 Shakespeare's Head. Shoppers in Carnaby Street seldom look
up beyond the flashing lights of the modish clothes shops. High
above them, surveying the scene with some astonishment, is a
lifelike bust of William Shakespeare. He might be about to utter
the words that he gave to King Lear: "I do not like the fashion of
your garments; you will say they are Persian attire, but let them be
changed."
Shakespeare's Head pub, Carnaby St, W1

An eloquent expression of gratitude is built into the
structure of Christ Church in Lambeth. A pattern of
stars and stripes on the tower is a perpetual reminder
that half the cost of the tower was borne by contri-
butions from America.

The Church of St Bride's off Fleet Street has the
tallest of Christopher Wren's spires, which is 226 feet
high. It is an extraordinary design, consisting of five
octagonal tiers, each one smaller than the tier below it.
Inevitably this has given rise to the legend that St
Bride's spire was the inspiration for the traditional
English wedding cake which also has several tiers. Of
course this legend is reinforced by the coincidence of St
Bride's name.

In the churchyard of St Mary at Hill, Billingsgate, is
a touching detail that reveals an architect's consideration for birds. When the offices overlooking the
churchyard were built, a copse of trees had to be cut
down which had contained a famous rookery. Sir
Henry Peak designed little nest boxes in the wall of his
new building so that the birds could be re-housed.
Unfortunately he knew little about the habits of the
rook, as this ungrateful bird will only settle in its own
clumsy nest of twigs.

You need never feel alone in the streets of central
London if you can enjoy the society of the amicable
lions, the cherubs and the animated old men that peer
down from so many walls and doorways. London's
most familiar lions are Sir Edwin Landseer's statues in
Trafalgar Square. The association of lions with the
centre of London is not as incongruous as it appears.
When the site of Drummond's Bank in Trafalgar
Square was excavated, the fossil bones of extinct
species of lions were discovered as well as those of bears
and tigers.

Cherubs were a characteristic architectural orna-
ment in the eighteenth century. Two cherubs are to be
seen playing a game of marbles on a fine carved wooden
canopy above the doorway of 1 Laurence Pountney
Hill in the City. They date from 1703. The facade of
the Royal Society of Arts, built by the Adam brothers
in 1774, is decorated with medallions of suitably
artistic cherubs. One of them is playing a harp, another
is sitting painting at an easel.

A statue of a cherub in the New Kent Road was put
up to turn a passage of Dickens' fiction into reality. In
David Copperfield Dickens described a statue in the
Kent Road as "...a great foolish image in the middle,
blowing on a dry shell." The image that Dickens

invented now exists – a chubby cherub blowing into a hollow shell.

When the Royal Automobile Club was built in Pall Mall in 1908–11 the pediment was adorned with a thoroughly modern cherub. It was shown at the wheel of the very latest motor car, now a vintage model that makes a delightful period piece. Slightly earlier than the motoring cherub are the marvellous tile paintings of early cars on the Michelin Tyre Company's building in the Fulham Road (see pages 18–9). High above the tiles, among the signs and decorations at roof level is the peculiar image of an early rubber tyre, permanently transfixed in the medium of stone.

In the City of London and nearby districts the boundaries of the separate parishes are marked by small plaques or carvings on the walls. These show simply the initials of the parish church with sometimes a crest and a date. One of the oldest parish boundary signs is a stone, at ground level, in Carey Street behind the Law Courts in the Strand. It is carved with an anchor which is the symbol of St Clement Danes and with SDW, representing St Dunstan in the West. Some parish boundaries can be seen in surprising places. One boundary passes through a public house, the George and Vulture off Lombard Street, and the boundary marks are on the wall above the bar. On Ascension Day several parishes keep up the tradition of beating the bounds when the choirboys and parishioners process around the parish boundaries (see page 25). One of the boundaries of St Clement Danes' parish is in the Thames and has to be reached by boat.

A rare survival from past times are small metal plaques called firemarks that are still to be seen on a few dwellings. Firemarks are embossed with pleasant images such as a phoenix, a handshake, or a figure of Britannia. They were issued by insurance companies to indicate that the householder was insured with them against fire, and they date from the days when fire engines were privately owned. If a house was on fire, but not insured, it was quite likely that the fire engine would not come to put it out.

Until the end of the eighteenth century the houses in London streets were not numbered, since only a small proportion of the population could read. Instead the streets were hung with innumerable carved and painted signs. These signs were used to distinguish between the houses in a street and to point out the shops, tradesmen's workshops and taverns. A typical address of the time was "At the Red Ball and Acorn, over and against the Globe Tavern in Queen Street." The modern equivalent would be quite simply 15 Queen Street, EC4.

The hanging signs were somewhat hazardous – horsemen were knocked off their mounts by signs swinging in the wind, and occasionally the metal supports broke and a heavy sign fell crashing on to some unfortunate pedestrian below. So it is not surprising that after the eighteenth century most of the trade signs were taken down. The whole idea of using symbols to denote trades is uncommon today but taverns still keep up the tradition with hanging pictorial signs. Several old trade signs can be seen in Lombard Street in the City for they were re-hung there outside the banks and offices as part of the decorations for the coronation of Edward VII in 1902. One sign shows a gilded cat playing a violin, which was a common theme among the traditional signs, especially for public houses. In fact originally the "cat and fiddle" had nothing to do with musical pets, but came from a corruption of the words "Caton le Fidele." The sign is a commemoration of a man called Caton who was a faithful knight at the time of Edward I.

Modern versions of some of the old trade signs are still fairly common. For instance the red and cream striped poles outside men's hairdressers' shops (the signs are sometimes neon-lit now, and revolved by electric motors) are relics of the days when barbers also acted as surgeons. They used to extract teeth and "bleed" patients (letting blood was thought to be a remedy for many disorders) – and this is the origin of their sign; the red stripes represent blood and the cream stripes are bandages. The meeting place of the Worshipful Company of Barbers is still known as Barber-Surgeons Hall, although they were separated from the Surgeons by Act of Parliament in 1745. A sign of three gold balls is traditional for the pawnbroker's

6 ∨

London lions
The lion is one of the commonest decorative themes on London buildings and this is probably due to its royal associations and its status as "king of the beasts." The lion made its first royal appearance around 1195 in the coat of arms of Richard I, crusader king who was known as "Coeur-de-Lion." Since then the three gold lions on a red background have been the Arms of England, and appear on the Royal crest. The lion also became associated with the iconography of empire, slumbering at the feet of wave-ruling Britannia. Rampant, couchant, guardant or as a head on a wall like some kind of hunting trophy of the British Raj, the lion is an ubiquitous denizen of the London streets.

6 This lion, and many like it, face the Thames and are normally well above high-water mark. It is said that when the lions drink, London must expect floods.
Below Victoria Embankment, WC2

7 *London Wall, EC2*

8 In memory of some mice
The nineteenth century building on the corner of Eastcheap and Philpot Lane is elaborately decorated with carvings. While the craftsmen were at work they were bothered by a plague of mice. This affectionate little carving shows the mice eating the men's lunch.
23–25 Eastcheap, City, EC3

<7   8∨

shop – and this originates from the Coat of Arms of the Medici family, which was one of the earliest families of bankers. The three balls are a departure from the original, as the Florentine family crest features no fewer than five balls, and instead of being gold they are coloured blue.

One pawnbroker's sign in London can be seen in a surprising place. It hangs above the bar in the Castle Inn in Cowcross Street, Clerkenwell, and it has been there since the days of George IV. The story goes that the king was spending a night out, incognito, and enjoying the plebeian pleasures of cock-fighting in Clerkenwell. He lost all his money on the betting, and he had no way to get back to the Palace. Luckily he still had his gold watch and he managed to persuade the landlord of the Castle to give him a loan against the security of the watch. The landlord obliged and, still unrecognized, the king went home to bed. The next morning a footman came to redeem the watch and presented the landlord with a royal warrant giving the inn keeper and his successors the right to act as pawnbrokers in perpetuity.

Some public clocks give periodic performances and provide mechanical sideshows in several streets. The clock at St Dunstan in the West, Fleet Street, dates from 1671 and is surmounted by the figures of the twin giants, Gog and Magog, who beat the bell with their clubs every quarter of an hour. Also on the quarter, at Liberty's shop off Regent Street, St George chases the dragon, but has not caught it yet. The bells of St Clement Danes church in the Strand fulfil the words of the nursery rhyme and play "oranges and lemons" at 9.0 am, noon, 3.00 pm and 6.00 pm.

One of the strangest clocks in London is aptly situated at the Eccentric Club in Ryder Street (not open to the public). The clock face is reversed from left to right and the hands travel anticlockwise. A barrel provides an apposite framework for a clock above Henekey's bar at 35 Strand. Another amusing image of time can be seen on the weather vane above the pavilion at Lord's cricket ground. It shows Father Time drawing stumps.

A fascinating modern clock covers one wall of Schroder Wagg's banking hall at 120 Cheapside. Made by Martin Burgess, the clock shows the time in different parts of the world. All the moving parts are exposed to view. A fine modern clock of traditional design can be seen above the door of the Financial Times offices in Cannon Street. In the centre of the dial is the face of Sir Winston Churchill.

Armed with his field guides to history and to architecture and with his binoculars to his eyes, the looker-up in London is a kind of urban birdwatcher. The rare specimens give a special thrill, but even the more common examples have their own beauty, and reveal their secrets to the patient seeker.

◁ 9

9 Ye Civet Cat. This ancient sign hangs somewhat incongruously over a bank. A tavern used to stand on the site long before the bank took it over.
Corner of High St and Church St, Kensington, W8

10 This gilded grasshopper hangs over the head offices of Martin's Bank. Founded in 1563 this bank is the oldest in England. The grasshopper was the emblem of Sir Thomas Gresham who lived in this house.
Martin's Bank, Lombard St, City, EC3

11 A grotesque dog, guarding one of the Guildhall chimneys.
Basinghall St, City EC2

12 The sun beams. This cheerful image is the symbol of an insurance company and provides a piece of light relief on a grey City facade. Gilded signs like this were common in eighteenth century London.
Basinghall Street, City, EC2

13 A goat eating a sprig of ivy is the symbol of the Huddersfield and Bradford Building Society.
200 Strand, WC2

10 ∧   11 ∧   12 ∨   13 ∨

PARIS-BORDEAUX
1895

PNE

14–20 The Michelin Building (1905–10) and some of its decorative panels. The artist has only recently been identified as Edouard Montaut (1879–1909) who also made lithographs of similar subjects. The liveliness of the paintings owes something to early photography – speed is conveyed by the blurred movements of the wheels and the slightly distorted perspective. They are classic evocations of the pleasures and excitements of pioneer motoring.
81 Fulham Rd, South Kensington, SW3

VOITURE sur MICHELIN

MICHELIN BOIT L'OBSTACLE

142

168

MADRID

GABRIE

MSCHILD

7

Trade signs
21 *55 New Oxford St, WC1*

22 A traditional trade sign marks the earlier site of a goldbeater's workshop. *Manette St, Soho, W1*

23 China tea only. The oriental gentlemen over the doorway of Twinings tea shop date from 1787. The tea plantations of India and Ceylon had not yet been laid out which explains why there are no Indians in the group – all tea came from China. *Twinings tea shop, Strand, WC2*

24 This curious sign which associates Britannia with a ring of Greek letters is the symbol of the Ionian Bank. This is a British bank, established in 1839 to service the Greek islands. The letters are the initials of the islands on which the first branches were opened. *Coleman St, City EC2*

22 ∧   21 ∧   23 ∨   24 ∨

Top hats

25 Four water babies in a boat. The wit of this unknown artist's advertisement equals that of familiar favourites Lewis Carroll and Edward Lear.
Carter's, Old Kent Rd, SE1

26 A charming sign for a little joke shop symbolizing the traditional conjurer's trick of producing rabbits from a hat.
Great Russell St, Bloomsbury, WC1

27 An enamel top hat, courteously raised above the door of a West End hat shop.
Jermyn St, St Jame's, SW1

◁25   26∧   27∨

Public clocks

28 A rebuke for meanness. This church clock has four faces, three of them white and illuminated at night, and one of them black and unlit. The white faces look towards the Borough district, where the residents contributed to a church appeal. The black face is a rebuke to the parisioners of Bermondsey who refused to give their charity.
St George's Church, Borough High St, SE1

29 A separate face. An unusual feature of this elegant clock is that the mechanism is inside the church some hundred feet away from the clock face, which it works by a system of levers.
St Mary at Hill, Billingsgate, EC3

29 ∧

30 ∨

30 A giant's pocket watch, in perfect working order, advertises a clockmaker's shop.
Holborn Viaduct, City, EC1

31 On the hour, the immaculate Mr Fortnum and Mr Mason glide out of their boxes, and bow to each other, as a carillon plays a tune. They founded the shop in 1707 but the clock was not put up until 1964.
Fortnum & Mason, Piccadilly, W1

28 ∧

31 ∨

32∧

32 A saucy shop clock of the 1930's, embellishing a highly respectable gentlemen's outfitters.
Alkit, Cambridge Circus, WC2

33∨

33 *Southampton St, WC2*

34 Another gentlemen's outfitters clock. This one raises its hat at midday.
Carter's, Old Kent Rd, SE1

34∨

London's living traditions

London does not hide her past away in museums and history books. History is re-enacted and celebrated in the streets, and the numerous customs and ceremonies that can be seen in the Capital provide a living link with her past.

London is a Royal City and many royal ceremonies serve to illustrate the relationship between Sovereign and State. Although for several generations the Monarch has been free from involvement with everyday politics, the Queen is still head of her Government. Each year in November, and after a General Election, London sees the pageantry of the State opening of Parliament, when the Queen travels by coach from Buckingham Palace to Westminster and takes her seat on the throne in the House of Lords. This ceremony has hardly changed since its inception in the mid-sixteenth century, and it still provides a graphic reminder of the Monarch's role. A few hours before the Queen arrives at Parliament, the Yeoman of the Guard search the cellars as they have done on every such occasion since Guy Fawkes tried to blow up Parliament on November 5th, 1605. Far from being a hollow ritual, this tradition has taken on a new meaning with political terrorism reappearing as a feature of modern life.

It is significant that the Queen opens Parliament from the Upper House, the Lords, and not from the Commons. In fact, no reigning Sovereign has entered the Commons for three and a quarter centuries, since Charles I came to arrest five members and was not allowed to do so. The will of the Commons cannot be violated even by the Monarch. Within Parliament, when the antagonism and tension of political debate threatens to disrupt proceedings, the calm rituals of ceremony and traditional etiquette serve to restore dignity and order. In the Commons the front benches of the two main political parties are still separated by a space that represents two sword lengths. The Speaker of the House of Commons is the arbiter of debate, and his authority is demonstrated at the opening of each day's business by his ceremonial procession through the Chamber, preceded by his mace of office. The Speaker's antiquated uniform of black knee-breeches, gown and wig segregate him from his colleagues and establish his authority among them. In just the same way the traditional robe and wig of the High Court judge symbolizes his authority over the Court.

The Stone of Scone is the seat upon which the ancient Kings of Scotland were crowned, and is the symbol of Scottish power. When Edward I conquered the Scots he wrested the Stone from them, brought it to London and in 1300 had the Coronation Chair built around it. Since then the Kings and Queens of England have been crowned while seated above this stone that symbolises their jurisdiction over Scotland.

Another symbolic seat is to be seen in the House of Lords. The Lord Chancellor presides over this House, from the "woolsack." This comfortable but informal throne has served for centuries as a constant reminder that the wealth of England was founded on wool.

In the House of Commons, Members of Parliament bow towards the Speaker's Chair when they enter the Chamber. Although it appears to demonstrate a healthy respect for the Chairman, this custom actually dates from the time when the Commons used to have St Stephen's Chapel as their meeting place, and an altar stood behind the Speaker's Chair. Members of the House of Commons in those days used to bow devoutly to the altar, and the custom has survived although the altar is no longer there.

The day's business at the House of Commons is closed with the call "Who goes home?" This colourful expression originates from the time when Members of Parliament used to travel home in groups as a protection against street thugs and highwaymen.

For many centuries much of the power and wealth of London was based within the City, which is the square mile centred around St Pauls. To a large extent London's wealth is still earned here, for the City is the centre of commerce. For centuries the City has had the power to run its own affairs, to elect its own leaders, to plan its own future. The City's own government is the Corporation, and at the Head of the Corporation is the Lord Mayor. Here again, the status and authority of the Lord Mayor is displayed with pageantry. The Lord Mayor's show has taken place each year in November for six hundred years. On this occasion the newly elected Mayor travels in the State coach through the City streets, followed by a procession of decorated floats illustrating themes that are relevant to the life and background of that particular Mayor. The Lord Mayor's coach, incidentally, is larger than the Queen's.

Traditionally the Sovereign herself respects the authority of the Lord Mayor within his own precincts, and whenever the Queen enters the City, she is met at the boundary by the Lord Mayor, who hands to her his

35 A trial without a prisoner

At the trial of the Pyx, a jury of independent experts assemble before a judge to test the quality of the coins of the realm that have been produced by the Royal Mint in the previous year. Trials of this kind date back to Anglo-Saxon times when the coinage was tested at regular intervals to make sure that it was not clipped or adulterated.

Today, one coin out of every 5,000 that are minted is placed in a sealed packet in a series of boxes called "The Pyx," which are brought to the Hall of the Goldsmiths' Company for the Trial. The jurymen check the number and denomination of the coins in each packet and then weigh the coins in bulk.

Another duty of the Goldsmith's Company, is the testing of the purity of the gold, silver and platinum used by silversmiths and jewellers. Any gold, silver or platinum object offered for sale in Britain must be stamped with a Hallmark. This name originally referred to the Mark applied at Goldsmiths' Hall.

36 Beating of the bounds

The Romans had a God of boundaries, called Terminus, in whose honour they used to process around their fields and make sacrifices for the protection of their crops. The Christian version of this ceremony is the "Beating of the bounds" which still takes place periodically in several London parishes. One of the most colourful processions starts from the Chapel Royal of St Peter ad Vincula within the Tower of London. The Chief Yeoman Warder of the Tower leads the choirboys around the 31 parish boundary marks in the surrounding streets. One of the marks is in the middle of a main road and the traffic is held up while the chaplain recites a prayer and the choirboys beat the mark vigorously with the willow wands that they carry. This part of the ritual stems from the time that the mass of the population was illiterate. Beating the boundary marks was the best way to impress them upon the parishioners' minds.

37 Parish boundaries
College Lane, City, EC4   37 ∨

35 ∧   36 ∨

sword of office, thereby symbolically transferring his authority to her. In his official life, the Lord Mayor goes nowhere in the City without his sword, and a unique feature of the City Churches are the brackets upon which many generations of Lord Mayors have rested the weight of their swords.

The right to elect the Lord Mayor of London and his officers, the Sheriffs, belongs to members of very ancient City institutions, the Livery Companies. The City Companies grew out of the trade guilds of the middle ages, and were responsible for maintaining the standards of trade within the City. Originally membership was restricted to practitioners of the particular trade, but in some Companies the connection has been lost, particularly in those like the Fan-makers, Gold and Silver Wyre Drawers' and Fletchers' (arrowmakers) where the craft itself has vanished from the City. However there are several Companies that still carry out their original duties, like the Fishmongers' Company which is responsible for testing the quality of fish brought in to London's Billingsgate Market, and the Apothecaries which provides an examining body for the pharmacist's profession. The Goldsmiths' Company manage the assay office where gold and silver is tested and Hall-marked, and the Company is also responsible for testing the nation's coinage as it comes from the Royal Mint.

The City Companies have a strict order of precedence. There are twelve chief Companies, led by the Mercers', the Grocers', the Drapers', the Fishmongers' and the Goldsmiths', in that order. Additionally there are no fewer than seventy four minor Companies. Predictably there has been some rivalry about precedence and in the early years the Companies seem to have competed for positions like football teams trying to get into the first division. One dispute gave rise to the expression "at sixes and sevens." This dates back to 1484 when the Skinners' and the Merchant Taylors' were jostling for sixth place in order of precedence; each unwilling to drop to seventh place. The argument was settled by the Lord Mayor of the day, who decreed that the Companies should change places every year.

At the banquets of some of the City Companies, guests drink a loving cup, and commemorate an event that took place in AD 978. In that year King Edward the Martyr was treacherously stabbed in the back by his mother in law, Elfrida, while he was drinking a cup of wine. To prevent a recurrence of this unsporting behaviour, each guest protects his neighbour as he drinks by standing with his back to him, guarding the rear.

After dinner at the Clothworkers' Company the waiters approach each guest with the surprising question "Do you dine, Sir, with Alderman or with Lady Cooper?" This is another way of offering brandy or gin. Legend has it that in the seventeenth century,

Alderman Cooper dined well as a guest of the Company, went home and promptly dropped dead. His wife, Lady Cooper accused the Clothworkers of over-indulging him with brandy. When she died herself, she left money in her will to provide gin for the Company's guests, as an alternative to their supposedly lethal beverage.

Many of London's surviving customs are modest and unostentatious affairs, that create a very personal link with people long dead. In 1346 Sir Robert Knollys built a small bridge in the City without first obtaining permission from the Lord Mayor. As a penalty he was

ordered to present a red rose to the Mayor every year on Midsummer's day, and his descendants continue the tradition to this day.

Some of London's customs are carried out behind closed doors, witnessed only by the participants and with the public excluded. Before reviling the London institutions for their exclusivity, one ought perhaps to reflect that it is only under these conditions that some traditions can remain alive. A living tradition does not depend upon spectators. Indeed an audience that does not participate can be harmful because it changes behaviour into an act, and real life into play-acting.

The election of the Lord Mayor
38 Guarding the wicket. Before the election of the Lord Mayor, a barrier known as the "wicket" is placed at the entrance to Guildhall. Only those entitled to vote, the Liverymen of the City Companies, are allowed through. There are different gates for members of the different Companies and the Company beadles stand at the gates nodding their members through. Here the beadle of the Plumbers' Company relaxes while the election proceeds inside.
Guildhall, Gresham St, EC2

39 A lady Alderman, accompanied by her Beadle, proceeds from church to the election of the Lord Mayor. There are 26 Aldermen of the City of London, each representing one of the City's divisions or "wards." Aldermen may stand for election as sheriffs, and subsequently may become Lord Mayor. London has yet to elect a Lady Mayor.
St Lawrence Jewry, EC2

40 City beadles who carry the Aldermen's maces.

41 ∧   42 ∨

41 A nose-gay for the Lord Mayor. A surprising detail of the costume of the Lord Mayor on election days is a little posy of flowers. Since the time of the plague in 1665–6 the Lord Mayor and City dignitaries have carried flowers on ceremonial occasions. The flowers were supposed to protect the bearer from the plague, and certainly a nosegay masked the stench of the City streets. By the same tradition, the Guildhall election platform, called the "hustings," is strewn with sweet smelling herbs at election time.
The Lord Mayor of London in 1975, Sir Murray Fox, at Guildhall

42 The Lord Mayor's entourage. On ceremonial occasions the Lord Mayor is preceded by the symbols of his authority, the Sword of State (dating from 1680) and the Great Mace (1735). The Lord Mayor's chain of office dates from the early sixteenth century. 1977 marks the election of the 650th Lord Mayor of London.
The Lord Mayor in 1976, Sir Lindsey Ring, at Guildhall

A procession of the Law

At the beginning of the law term in early October, Her Majesty's Judges and Queens' Councillors attend a service at Westminster Abbey. Afterwards the Lord Chancellor leads the procession across the road to a reception at the House of Lords.

43 Purple-trimmed robes are worn by County Court Judges.

44 Red robes distinguish Judges of the Queen's Bench Division.

45 The most senior Judges, who adjudicate at the Court of Appeal, have gold trimmings on their robes, and are assisted by pages.

43∧   45∨

44∧

46 The Quit Rents Ceremony

The lawyer is the solicitor of the Corporation of London. He is demonstrating to an assembled company that a billhook is not capable of cutting a bundle or "faggot" of wood. He will then try the same experiment with an axe; this time he will cut through the wood with a single blow. This extraordinary ritual is part of a ceremony that dates back at least 775 years. A blunt billhook and a sharp axe are paid annually as rent for a piece of land in Shropshire, the exact whereabouts of which have been forgotten. By paying this rent to a legal officer of the Crown, known as the Queen's Remembrancer, the City Corporation are "Quitted", or relieved, of their obligation for a year. A second "Quit Rent" is paid, this time for a blacksmith's forge that stood beside the Knights Templars' jousting ground in the parish of St Clement Danes. In 1235 King Henry III gave the blacksmith Walter le Brun, rights to the land, in exchange for a rent of six horseshoes and sixty-one nails. The horseshoes and nails that are counted out and exchanged each year are at least 550 years old. To assist him with his counting the City solicitor places the nails on a chequered tablecloth – thus giving a graphic demonstration of the origin of the word "Exchequer."

The Royal Courts of Justice, Strand, WC2

46∨

47∧

47 Commemorating a London historian

The memorial to John Stow has a real quill pen in its hand. Every year the Lord Mayor or his representative gives the historian a new pen, as a tribute to the continuing value of his writings. Stow published his *Survey of London* in 1598 when he was seventy-three years old. A poor man, a tailor, he had lived through the most destructive period of the Reformation. He made it his life's work to record the London that he had known. His *Survey* is one of the foundations of all later histories of London.
St Andrew Undershaft, Leadenhall St, EC3

The Mounting of the Queen's Life Guard

48 At 10.30 each morning the Queen's Life Guard leaves the Knightsbridge Barracks of the Household Cavalry to mount the Guard in Whitehall at 11.00. The leader of the troop blows a bugle call, the sentry at the gate salutes, and the horses clatter down through Hyde Park.
10.30 am Park gate, Knightsbridge Barracks, SW7

49 A policeman holds up the traffic at Hyde Park as the Queen's Life Guard pass the Wellington Arch. The equestrian statue is of the Duke of Wellington on his charger Copenhagen, a horse that the iron Duke buried with full military honours at his country estate. When this bronze statue was erected no less than forty horses were needed to drag it into position.
10.35 am Hyde Park Corner, SW1

48∧   49∨

50, 51 Oak Apple Day

Recently arrived pensioners at the Royal Hospital in Chelsea get a surprise early in June when they find that the statue of their founder, King Charles II, has been swathed up to the neck with oak branches. "What have they done to our Charley-boy?" one of them was heard to remark affectionately. The decoration of the statue is part of the celebration of Oak Apple Day, and commemorates King Charles' escape after the Battle of Worcester in 1651 when he hid from his pursuers in the branches of an oak tree.

After the inspection and the march-past, the Governor of the hospital leads the pensioners in raising their hats for three rousing cheers for their pious founder, Charles II, and three more cheers for Her Majesty the Queen.

50 ∧

51 >

53 The Square lit by candlelight
On Christmas Eve, something of the atmosphere of old London is re-created at Campden Hill Square in Kensington, when the residents put three candles in each of their windows and extinguish all other lights. Carol singers sing in the street by lantern light.

54 A traditional bunfight
Shrove Tuesday is a day of indulgence in the Christian calendar. This is the last day before Lent, and Christians traditionally feed themselves up before the long fast. Shrove Tuesday was the day on which cooks were supposed to finish off the last of their fat, and this is the origin of the traditional English dish, the pancake, and of an ancient ceremony called the Pancake Greaze at Westminster School. The school was founded in 1560, and the light-hearted custom is several hundred years old. The school chef cooks a pancake, and carries it ceremoniously into the School Hall, where all the boys and masters are assembled, as well as the Dean and Chapter of Westminster Abbey. The chef tosses the pancake over a high bar, and as it falls, a group of boys fight for the pieces. The battle lasts for a minute, after which time the pieces are weighed and the boy with the largest wins a golden guinea.

52 Trooping the Colour
London's most colourful royal pageant originates from a relatively mundane military tradition. British Army regiments used to parade at nightfall and the regimental colours were carried through the ranks before being lodged for the night at the regimental headquarters. The purpose of this was simply to make sure that the men would recognize their own colours. Since 1755 the Trooping of the Colour has been held at the Horse Guards' Parade as a purely ceremonial occasion. It is performed on the Queen's official birthday in June and the seven regiments of the Household Division provide a dazzling display.

53∧

52∨

54∨

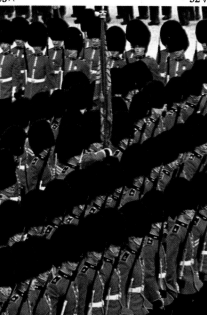

56 ∧

55, 56 Underneath the arch
Once a fortnight the children of Bow in the East End of London make their way towards a small wooden arch set up on the pavement, with the inscription "Enter all ye children small. None can come who are too tall." Any child small enough to pass without touching the arch is given a parcel or "bundle" of toys, in exchange for a halfpenny. This charity was started early this century when there was great poverty in the district. The arch has now been raised by several inches to make up for the increased height of today's better-fed children.
Fern St, E3

57 Hanging the bun
Ceremonies develop into cheerful occasions, even if they commemorate sad events. Some two hundred years ago a widow, whose only son was a sailor, expected him home for Easter and kept a hot-cross bun to celebrate his return. He never came, and she never received news of his fate. Each year until she died she baked a bun in his memory and kept the buns from past years. A pub, built on the site of her cottage, came to be called "The Widow's Son." Here, every Good Friday, a sailor adds a new bun to the collection that hangs over the bar. Black, shrunken and dusty with age, they provide a curious memorial to a widow's sorrow.
Devons Rd, Bow, E3

<55   57 ∨

Pearly Kings and Queens

The Victorian and Edwardian periods are seen now as a highpoint of English history, when everything seemed to go right. The British Empire embraced the world. The middle classes accumulated wealth and property. The railways straddled the land, bringing Aberdeen and Aberystwyth only a day away from London. English literature blossomed. Architects confidently adjusted the buildings of past centuries to fit in with their own theories. After such peaks every subsequent step often appears to be downhill.

But there was a dark shadow behind the highlights of Victorian and Edwardian achievement. At the back of the puffed-up prosperity, the success, the stability of those times was an ever-present wound – the pain and poverty of the ordinary people. Poverty does not erect memorials to itself; history washes over it like the tide.

Nowhere was the poverty worse than in London. With agriculture becoming mechanized, fewer workers were needed on the land and country people fled to the cities to find work. In London the population was swollen by immigrants too. The Irish came to escape the potato famine of 1846–8. Between 1880 and 1914 some 100,000 Jewish refugees from Tsarist persecution in Russia settled in the East End.

Men, women and children took to the streets to find work. They played music, danced with bears, sold matches, toffee apples, flypapers, flowers or fruit. The most successful street pedlars graduated to the ownership of a market stall, and to the ancient title of "costermonger."

Literally, a costermonger is a seller of apples. "Monger" means vendor and "costard" was a word used in the thirteenth century for a particular kind of large cooking apple. A large proportion of costermongers were fruit sellers, but the name came to apply to any street market stallholder.

Henry Mayhew, the chronicler of the lives of London's poor in the nineteenth century, calculated that there were an average of fourteen street stalls per mile throughout London in 1851, representing a grand total of some 30,000 costermongers. Writing in 1861, he described the costermongers' dress:

"A well-to-do 'coster' when dressed for the day's work, usually wears a small cloth cap, a little on one side . . . Coats are seldom indulged in; their waistcoats, which are of a broad-ribbed corduroy, with fustian back and sleeves, being made as long as a groom's and buttoned up nearly to the throat . . . If the cord be of a dark ratskin hue, then mother of pearl buttons are preferred . . . The man who does not wear his silk neckerchief – his 'King's man' as it is called – is known to be in desperate circumstances . . . Even if a costermon-

ger has two or three silk handkerchiefs by him already he seldom hesitates to buy another, when tempted with a bright showy pattern hanging from a Field-lane doorpost.''

Already the costermonger was a bit of a dandy, his dress reflecting his status as king of the street. But soon the decorative mother-of-pearl buttons, a fashionable accessory among the middle classes at the time, were to assume another role in the street markets. There was bitter rivalry between costermongers for the best pitches in the streets. Shopkeepers joined in the fray, as the costermongers took away their trade. It was a free-for-all as the street stalls were not licensed or controlled. Relations between the costermongers and police were bad, and somebody was needed to arbitrate between the factions. From among the costermongers themselves, leaders came forward who commanded the respect of all the traders in a street. As a mark of their authority, they wore one or two rows of the fashionable pearl buttons on their caps, and this made them easy to recognize in a busy street. In this way the Pearly Kings were born.

With their natural inclination for flashy dress it was not long before the kings of the costermongers began to extend their rows of pearl buttons. It was around 1880 that a Pearly King first appeared dressed from head to toe in pearl buttons. His name was Henry Croft; his tomb in Finchley Cemetery has a life-size figure of him in his pearly suit. With this over-loaded costume the Pearly Kings, and their Queens, began to take on a new role in their communities. Their costume made them the centre of attention at street carnivals and bazaars. The publicity that they attracted made them ideal collectors for charity.

There was no Welfare State, no dole, no National Health. The welfare of the needy in the poor districts of London was left largely to the charitable and church institutions. The Pearly Kings and Queens, working still as costermongers during the day, put on their costumes in their spare time and travelled around their Boroughs, collecting for the local good causes. This is the role that they have maintained to this day.

The Pearlies are family institutions. Several Pearly Families have dynasties that have already extended to five generations. Kings, Queens, Princes and Princesses are all entitled to wear pearl buttons, and they can sew them in whatever patterns they wish. There is only one Pearly family for any London Borough. Succession is by inheritance, but the rules are flexible. If the heir does not want to become King, then somebody else can be appointed instead.

58 A Pearly Queen at the Costermongers' Harvest Festival, *St Martin's in the Fields, Trafalgar Sq, SW1.*

59 ∧

60 ∨

The Pearly Royalty

59–62 The Pearly Kings and Queens of London get together once a year for one big jovial jamboree. Each monarch brings offerings of fruit, flowers and vegetables to the Costermongers' Harvest Festival at St Martin's in the Fields in early October. The Vicar of St Martin's is an honorary pearly for the day. He wears a stole with pearl buttons. Five generations of one family, the Marriotts, are here, all in pearly costume. The different clans greet each other like brothers and sisters all of one family. Chelsea and Stoke Newington embrace. Lambeth and Whitechapel get together for a chat. East meets West; all London is united in London's own particular style of cockney fellowship.

59 One Pearly Prince brings a pumpkin.

60 A small boy finds his harvest offering too tempting to resist.

61∧

62∨

63 On the way to his own execution St Blaise saved the life of a child who was choking on a fishbone. On St Blaise's Day, a priest blesses children's throats. *St Ethelreda's Church, Ely Place, EC1*

64 Blessing the fish. At the fishermen's harvest festival near Billingsgate, the priest blesses a display of some thirty five kinds of fish. *St Mary at Hill, Billingsgate, EC3*

SOME LONDON CEREMONIES AND EVENTS

Bold figures in brackets refer to illustrations

JANUARY

6th Royal Epiphany. 11.30 am the Queen, accompanied by her Yeomen of the Guard, attends service at the Chapel Royal in St James's Palace. Three purses, symbolizing the gifts of gold, frankincense and myrrh, are presented, and later distributed to the poor of the parish.

6th Baddeley cake. Unsuccessful actor Robert Baddeley (died 1795) bequeathed money to provide a Twelfth Night cake and wine for the cast at Drury Lane Theatre, after the night's performance.

30th Anniversary of Charles I's execution. Wreaths are laid beneath his statue at Charing Cross.

FEBRUARY

3rd Blessing of the throats (63).
6th Elizabeth's II's accession. Anniversary salute of 41 guns in Hyde Park by the King's Troop of the Royal Horse Artillery, and at the Tower of London by the Honourable Artillery Company. Salutes are also fired on April 21st (Queen's birthday), June 2nd (Prince Philip's birthday), the 2nd Saturday in June (Queen's official birthday) and August 4th (Queen Mother's birthday).

16th (about) Chinese New Year. Celebrated in Gerrard St, Soho, W1.

Shrove Tuesday. Pancake Greaze (54). *By special invitation of the Headmaster.*

Late Feb. **The Trial of the Pyx (35).** *By invitation of the Goldsmiths Company.*

Middle of Lent. **Mothering Sunday.** At a service at the Chapel Royal in the Tower of London children receive flowers and simnel cakes, traditional fare on this day since Tudor times.

MARCH

21st Vernal equinox. Druids gather on Tower Hill.

Late March. **Oranges and lemons service.** St Clement Danes church, Strand, WC2, at 3 pm, after which fruit is distributed to children, celebrating the famous rhyme.

APRIL

About 6th **John Stow service (47).**

Good Friday. **Hanging the bun (57).**

Good Friday. **Butterworth Charity.** Under an ancient bequest 21 poor widows of the parish of St Bartholomew the Great, Smithfield, EC1, should receive a hot-cross bun and sixpence at the tomb of their benefactor. This part of London is so depopulated that there is not a single widow left; so the charity is distributed among any children that attend.

Easter Sunday. **Church Parade at the Tower of London.** Yeomen warders parade in state dress for inspection by the Resident Governor, before morning service at the Chapel Royal. They also parade on Whit Sunday and on the Sunday before Christmas.

Easter Monday. **Harness Horse Parade.** A rally of traditional brewers' drays and immaculate carts and carriages, Regent's Park, NW1 9.45 am to noon.

Around Easter **The Boat Race.** Crews from Oxford and Cambridge Universities row 4 miles 374 yards from Putney to Mortlake. First rowed in 1856.

20th John Cass Service (80).

Last Sunday **Roman Catholic Pilgrimage.** Follows the route taken by reformation martyrs from Newgate Prison (Newgate St, EC1) to Tyburn gallows (Marble Arch).

MAY

Ascension Day **Beating the bounds (36).**

Late May **Chelsea Flower Show (222).**

29th (about) Oak Apple Day (50–1). *Tickets by application.*

Last Wednesday **Pepys service.** Church of St Olave, Hart St, EC3.

JUNE

Early June **Beating of the Retreat.** Military pageant on Horseguards Parade (3 consecutive evenings). *Ticket Centre, 1b Bridge St, SW1.*

2nd Saturday **Trooping of the Colour.** Queen's official birthday (52). *Ticket Centre, 1b Bridge St, SW1.*

24th Midsummer Day **Presentation of the Knollys Rose** (see page 26). Picked beside All Hallows Church, Barking, but presented in private.

24th **City of London Election** of two Sheriffs, the Chamberlain, Bridge Masters Ale Conners and Auditors.

65, 66 The Order of Bards, Ovates and Druids celebrates the Autumn Equinox and harvest. One child, called the *habin*, presents a wheatsheaf. Another child carries the horn of plenty, a cow's horn

containing wine. King Arthur's sword is carried in procession. Fruit is scattered on the ground and peace invoked. The chosen chief and Pendragon, his second in command, give a poetry reading.

Parliament Hill Fields, NW3 : a different group of Druids assemble at Primrose Hill.

Guildhall at noon. *Spectators may view by application at the Guildhall.*

29th **St Peter's Day.** In 616 AD a fisherman is said to have rowed a stranger across the Thames to Thorney Island, site of Westminster Abbey. The stranger revealed himself to be St Peter and told the man to cast his net the following day and present the salmon that he caught to the Bishop of London. The Fishmongers' Company presents a salmon to the Dean and Chapter of the Abbey to commemorate the legend.

JULY
Thursday after 4th **Procession of the Vintner's Company.** 4 pm (**1**).
3rd week. **Swan-upping.** Crews set out from Temple Steps, Embankment on Monday 9.30 am (**230**)
Late July **Doggett's Coat and Badge Race.** The oldest race on the river (**254**).
Late July–September **Henry Wood Promenade concerts**.

SEPTEMBER
About 21st **Christ's Hospital School Service.** Boys march, in traditional uniform of blue cassocks and yellow socks, from London Bridge Station to St Sepulchre's, High Holborn for St Matthew's Day service at 3 pm, led by the school band.
29th Michaelmas Day **Election of Lord Mayor.** Guildhall at noon (**38**).

OCTOBER
1st **Opening of Law Term.** Judges Service at Westminster Abbey (about

11.30 am) and procession (**43–5**).
1st Sunday. **Costermongers' Harvest Festival.** 3.30 pm (**58–62**).
2nd Sunday **Harvest of the Sea** (**64**).
21st **Trafalgar Day.** Wreaths laid at Nelson's Column, Trafalgar Sq, WC2.
Late Oct. **Quit Rents Ceremony** (**46**).
By invitation of the Queen's Remembrancer.

NOVEMBER
1st Sunday **London to Brighton Vintage Car Rally.** Vintage and veteran cars leave Hyde Park Corner from 8 am to attempt the 60 mile run.
Early Nov. **State Opening of Parliament.** The Queen rides in the Irish State Coach from Buckingham Palace to the House of Lords.
5th **Guy Fawkes Night.** Fireworks and bonfires celebrate his failure to blow up King and Parliament in 1605.
2nd Saturday **Lord Mayor's Show.** A procession, with floats, each year on a different theme, through City streets. The new Lord Mayor rides from Guildhall to the Law Courts to take the oath before the Lord Chief Justice.
2nd Sunday **Remembrance Sunday.** At a parade of all the Services in Whitehall the Queen, Prime Minister and Commonwealth High Commissioners lay wreaths on the Cenotaph and lead the nation in remembering the fallen. Two minutes silence is observed as Big Ben strikes 11 o'clock.

DECEMBER
10th–January 6th **Christmas Tree,**

presented by the people of Norway, decorates Trafalgar Square.

DAILY THROUGH THE YEAR
Changing of the Guard. Buckingham Palace, SW1. 11.30 am. When the Queen is not in residence the ceremony takes place at St James's Palace, SW1.
Mounting the Queen's Life Guard. Horse Guards Arch, Whitehall, SW1, 11.00 am. (**48–9**).
Ceremony of the Keys. Tower of London, EC3, 9.50 pm. The Chief yeoman warder locks up the Tower for the night and, doffing his bonnet, calls out "God preserve Queen Elizabeth." *Tickets on written application.*
Speaker's Procession. House of Commons, SW1, 2.28 pm. Proceeded by his chaplain and macebearer, Mr Speaker walks through the lobby on his way to open the day's debate. This is the only occasion that English policemen on duty raise their helmets in salute. *Apply to the police officers on duty.*

FORTNIGHTLY
Alternate Fridays. **"Farthing Bundles."** Fern St, Bow, E3, 8.45 am (**55–6**).

The dates of many events vary from year to year, particularly those associated with Easter. For up-to-date information contact *London Tourist Board, 4 Grosvenor Gns, SW1.*

Street furniture and memorials

The joy of sauntering at leisure along city streets is immeasurably increased when one encounters ordinary functional things that are well designed and distinctive. Lamp posts, letter boxes and public benches exist primarily to serve a useful purpose but they can do more than this. They can have an inspired elegance and a quality of craftsmanship that raises them above function to art. Some street furniture too, by virtue of its survival from an earlier age, serves as a capsule of social history, giving insights into life in times past.

Statues and memorials are not subservient to function to the extent that lamp posts and park benches are. They can perform purely as art and they commemorate history more directly and deliberately. England cannot lay claim to sculptors of the calibre of Michelangelo and Cellini, whose works can be seen in Florence's squares, but London does boast public works by most of the best sculptors that have worked here. Le Sueur's figure of Charles I (1633) at Charing Cross is one of the finest equestrian portraits in any city. The magnificent Grinling Gibbons is well represented by his figures of James II in front of the National Gallery and of Charles II at the Royal Hospital, Chelsea.

Jacob Epstein, a giant but controversial figure in twentieth-century sculpture, stands up well when judged by the head of William Blake at Poets' Corner in Westminster Abbey, and by the Madonna and Child of 1952 in Cavendish Square. Henry Moore, who in 1929 shared with Epstein in the decoration of the London Transport Headquarters in Broadway SW1, carved a distinguished stone parapet at the new Time-Life building in New Bond Street. Several of his later sculptures have recently appeared in London, seeming paradoxically like great rocks that have lain undisturbed for millenia. Good examples can be seen near the Jewel Tower at Westminster and on Millbank beside Vauxhall Bridge.

Lovers of the incongruous and the bizarre will find plenty to amuse them among London's huge collection of monuments. London's first nude male statue was commissioned with unwonted immodesty by the women of England. It was the figure of Achilles, set up in honour of the Duke of Wellington, at the south eastern corner of Hyde Park in 1822. Seeing it for the first time a veteran of Napoleon's defeated armies was heard to mutter "Vengeance at last."

The men of the British Army enjoyed a certain vengeance over their Commander in Chief, Frederick Augustus, Duke of York who was held up to some ridicule in the nursery rhyme for having "had ten thousand men. He marched them up to the top of the hill and he marched them down again." The Duke's unpopularity probably dates from 1833 when his statue and column in Waterloo Place, St James's, was paid for by stopping one day's wages from every officer and man in the British Army. It was said that the Duke needed the pedestal, 124 feet high, to escape from his creditors and that the lightning conductor on top would make a convenient spike for his bills.

Queen Boadicea, by Westminster Bridge, is driving her chariot horses without benefit of reins. Captain Cook in the Mall is shown in an unseamanlike position – standing on a coil of rope. One of London's best known statues, at the centre of Piccadilly Circus, is mistakenly known as "Eros." The figure, by Sir Alfred Gilbert (1893), was set up as a memorial to the Earl of Shaftesbury. It was intended to represent the Angel of Christian Charity and, as a veiled pun on the philanthropist's name, the Angel seems to have shot an arrow, so that the shaft is buried in the ground.

There is touching evidence of nineteenth century morality in the Square beside Smithfield Market. Here there is a bronze statue of a nude lady who was intended to symbolise Peace. However, she was widely thought to represent Fertility – and as such it was thought to indicate that the lady was married. So when a gold ring was found nearby, it was attached to the finger of the sculpture, putting many troubled minds at rest.

When he died in 1832, Jeremy Bentham bequeathed his skeleton to University College, of which he was one of the founders. In his Will he directed that the skeleton should be dressed in his cloth coat, nankeen trousers, woollen socks and slippers, seated on a cane chair and boxed in a mahogany and glass case. Thus he sits, in a university corridor, like a benign hall porter in his lodge, London's most disconcerting memorial.

67 The last of the lamplighters. The gas lamps at the Temple are still lit every day by hand. Ivan Ramnauth has been employed for twenty years by the gas board as the only lamplighter in London. His round takes him an hour, and he comes back every morning to turn the lamps off. In 1962 Mr Ramnauth flew to Seattle to light the flame of the World fair.
At dusk : Middle Temple, Fleet St, EC4

69 ∧

68 ∧

70 ∨

Lamp posts

68 A cherub on the telephone. He is listening through one of the old receivers that were in use in 1895 when the lamp post was put up. A companion figure is talking into the 'phone. The lamps, with their unusual figures, flank the doorway of the town house of the first Lord Astor.
Temple Place, Embankment, WC2

69 An animated group, whose postures have been frozen in cast iron for nearly a century.
Cheyne Walk, Chelsea, SW3

70 A corpulent cherub on the pedestal of a lamp.
Trinity Sq, Tower Hill, EC3

71 At each corner of the square in which Nelson's monumental column stands are the lamps that came from his flagship HMS *Victory*. Originally oil lamps, they were converted first to gas and then to electricity. Lamplighters were given extra wages for cleaning them as they are so large. Another little-known feature of the square are the imperial standards of length, from one inch to one hundred feet, which were set up under the north parapet in 1876.
Trafalgar Sq, SW1

71 ∨

72 The camel is not a very apt symbol for comfortable seating, but here it makes the most distinctive street furniture in London.
Seat on the Victoria Embankment, WC2

73 The dolphin is a mammal and not one that frequents the Thames. But it is widely used as a fishy Thameside symbol, and even appears in the Arms of the Fishmongers' Company.
Lamp post : Victoria Embankment, WC2

74 *Victoria Embankment, WC2*

75 ∧

Charity children
Before the days of free State schools,
poorer children used to go to schools run
by the Church or by Charities. Many of the
Charity Schools could be identified by the
charming carvings of boys and girls which
decorated their facades. Some of these are
carved from wood, and some made from a
unique material called Coade stone. This is
an extremely hard synthetic stone, made to
a secret formula which has been lost. At the
Coade factory in Lambeth, opened in
1769, Charity children were made for
sixteen guineas a pair.

75 Charity boy.
St Andrew's Church, Holborn, EC1

76 A pair of Charity children.
*Behind St Mary Abbot's Church,
Kensington Church St, W8*

77, 78 When it was run by charity,
Greycoats School was for boys and girls,
and so male and female charity children
appear above the door. The School is now
for girls only.
Greycoats Place, Westminster, SW1

76 ∧   77 ∨   78 ∨

79 ∧

79 Charity girl.
St Andrew's Church, Holborn, EC1

80, 81 A charity girl seen in context and in detail, above Sir John Cass school.
Sir John Cass, a benefactor to the City in many ways, died in 1718 of an haemorrhage while signing his will and the quill was stained with blood. Children of this school attend an annual service on the anniversary wearing red feathers in his memory.
Sir John Cass School, Aldgate, E1

Charity figures can also be seen at the following addresses:
St Botolph's Church Hall, Bishopsgate, EC2 (see page 6)
43 Hatton Garden, Holborn, EC1
Vintners' Place, Upper Thames St EC4
Blewcoats School, Caxton St, Westminster, SW1
St Luke's School, Old St, Clerkenwell, EC1
St Mary's School, Rotherhithe St, SE16

80 ∨

81 ∨

82 ∧

84 ∨

83 ∧

85 ∧

86 ∨

Royal portraits

82 A bust of Charles I, marking the site of his execution.
Banqueting House, Whitehall, SW1
An almost identical bust can be seen on the east wall of St Margaret's Church, Westminster. The best statue of Charles I is the equestrian portrait by le Sueur at Charing Cross. Cast in 1633, it was removed during the Commonwealth and sold to a brazier called Rivett to be melted down. He did a brisk trade in souvenirs, allegedly made from the metal of the statue, but actually was a Royalist and hid the sculpture triumphantly producing it again at the restoration of the monarchy in 1660.

83 George I. Incongruously dressed in Roman costume, George I surmounts the stepped spire of this handsome church designed by Nicholas Hawksmoor.
St George's, Bloomsbury Way, WC1

84 The head of the boy king, Edward VI. This portrait is a detail of a building put up in 1805 but it marks the site of Edward's palace, Bridewell, which he endowed as a hospital. It later became a dreaded prison.
New Bridge St, City, EC4

85 This marble statue of Queen Victoria is by her own daughter, Princess Louise. Dated 1893, it is a very competent if uninspired piece of carving. Behind the statue is Kensington Palace, the house in which, when barely eighteen years old, Victoria was woken at six o'clock on a cold morning in June 1837 to be told of her accession to the throne by Lord Conyngham and the Archbishop of Canterbury.
Kensington Gardens, W8

86 Queen Anne has stood here since 1708, although the statue was made for the portico of St Mary-le-Strand Church.
Queen Anne's Gate, Westminster, SW1

87 Mary Queen of Scots, dwarfed by the lettering of the newspaper that occupies the building.
143 Fleet St, EC4

88 The only surviving figure of the Queen Elizabeth I that was carved in her own lifetime. Dating from 1586, the statue originally stood over one of the great gates into the City, Ludgate, and it came through the Fire of London unscathed.
St Dunstan's in the West, Fleet St, EC4

89∧

92∨

93∨

94∨

95∑

89 These two incongruous slabs of stone were placed here at the request of the Duke of Wellington so that he could mount his horse more comfortably.
Outside the Athenaeum Club, Pall Mall, SW1

90 The gentle image of a pet dog conflicts with the function of the object which it decorates – a war cannon.
Inside the Tower of London, EC3

91 The porter's rest. This shoulder-high slab of wood was erected in 1861 by the vestry of St George's Church, Hanover Square "for the benefit of porters and others carrying burdens."
Piccadilly, (South, near Hyde Pk Corner), W1

92 Recycling the refuse of war. Many bollards on London pavements are made from ships' cannons, discarded after various 18th and early 19th century campaigns and surmounted by cannon-balls. This re-cycling process was reversed in the last war, when iron railings from London streets and squares were melted down to make weapons.
Winchester Square, Bankside, SE1

93 *St John St, Clerkenwell, EC1*

94 False cannon bollard of 1909.
Waterloo Place, St James's, SW1

95 A memorial to a pantomime cat: the Whittington Stone. Although Sir Richard Whittington existed and was three times Lord Mayor of London, in 1398, 1407 and 1420, his cat is a fiction. The legend that it was responsible for his success probably grew from the belief that he made his fortune from coal: coal barges were known as "cats." At this spot, as a poor young man leaving London, Whittington is supposed to have heard Bow Bells five miles away, calling "turn again."
Highgate Hill, N6

MORE UNUSUAL MONUMENTS

Prince Albert (1873 by Charles Bacon) at Holborn Circus, EC1, has been called London's most polite statue; he is raising his hat.
Sir Sydney Waterlow, in Waterlow Park, Highgate Hill, N6, is the most prudent; he is carrying an umbrella. **Lord Palmerston** (1876 by Thomas Woolner) in Parliament Square, SW1 is the best dressed; Desmond MacCarthy wrote of it "It ought to be an object of pilgrimage to all the tailors in England. The frockcoat fits like a glove, and though the trousers do not break on the instep enough to suit modern taste, the hang of them is magnificent." **William Huskisson** in Pimlico Gardens, SW1 is less well dressed. As the first victim of the Railway Age (he died under a train in 1830) he is most unsuitably draped in a revealing Roman toga. He looks, as Osbert Sitwell wrote, like "Boredom rising from the bath".
William III on horseback (J. Bacon 1807) stands in St James's Square, SW1. The molehill is shown, which tripped his horse, killing the king. After this accident, the king's enemies used to drink to the health of "the little gentleman in velvet." Two equestrian statues by Sir Francis Legatt Chantrey show famous men riding without boots, saddles or stirrups. They are **George IV** in the north-eastern corner of Trafalgar Square, SW1 and the **Duke of Wellington** at the Royal Exchange, EC3.
Florence Nightingale in Waterloo Place, SW1 is holding an oil lamp instead of the legendary candle lantern that she carried in the Crimea.
London's oldest outdoor statue is probably the figure of the Egyptian God, **Sekhmet**, which presides over the entrance to Sotheby's in Bond Street. **Cleopatra's Needle**, on the Embankment near Charing Cross, WC2, has no connection with the Egyptian queen. It dates from about 1450 BC and was one of a pair erected by Thothmes III in front of a sun temple. In 23 BC the Emperor Augustus took the obelisks to Alexandria, and in 1877 one of them was brought by sea to London (the other went to New York). Two large jars within the pedestal contain an assortment of oddities, including a standard pound weight, a case of cigars, a box of hairpins, a copy of "The Times" for the day that the obelisk was set up, a portrait of Queen Victoria and Bradshaw's Railway Guide.
The **London Stone**, set into a wall of the Bank of China in Canon Street, EC4 is thought to have been the Roman "milliarium," from which road distances from London were measured.

96 ∧

97 ∨

96 Marx's grave
Pilgrims from all over the world leave flowers at Karl Marx's grave. Marx lived in Dean Street, Soho, and did research for *Das Kapital* in the Reading Room of the British Museum. There is rivalry among readers to use the desk that he habitually occupied.
Marx's grave : Highgate Cemetary, N6

97 Commemorating the Great Fire
This little statue, known as the golden boy of Cock Lane, used to have an inscription which read "This boy is in memory put up of the late Fire of London, occasioned by the sin of gluttony 1666." The mention of gluttony is an oblique reference to the fact that the fire began in Pudding Lane and ended here at Pie Corner.
Cock Lane, EC1

98 William Shakespeare
A lad from the country who found fame in London. This memorial marks the site of the Globe Playhouse, built in 1599 by the company of players to which he belonged and for which many of his plays were written. Constructed mainly from the timber of their previous Theatre north of the Thames, it caught fire in 1613 during a performance of "Henry VIII." Rebuilt, it survived until 1644.
Park St Bankside, Southwark, SE1
On the opposite side of the river is Playhouse Yard where the Blackfrairs Theatre stood; an indoor playhouse (the Globe was open to the sky) where such plays as "The Tempest," requiring more elaborate effects were presented. "The Comedy of Errors" had its first performance in the Hall of Gray's Inn in 1594 and the Hall of Middle Temple was the venue for the opening of "Twelfth Night" on February 2nd 1602.

99 An honourable war wound
The figure on the right represents America and its arm was blown off by a bomb in 1944. It came to symbolise America's sacrifice in the war – until 1977 when an American company subscribed to have the arm replaced.
Bush House, Aldwych, WC2

100 This elegant figure was put up above a jeweller's shop in 1883, and represents the young lady in Byron's poem "Lara". She owes her position here to the jeweller's pun on Byron's lines:
> They were not common links that formed the chain
> That bound to Lara, Kaled's heart and brain.

Gold chains, of course, were a profitable line for jewellers in the 1880's.
George Attenborough & Son, 193 Fleet St, EC4

98 ∧   99 ∨   100 ∨

The public face

In September 1666, four-fifths of the medieval jumble of streets in the City of London were destroyed by fire. The Great Fire burnt for five days and consumed some 13,200 homes as well as St Paul's Cathedral and 88 of the City's 108 churches.

With this disaster came London's great chance to reshape the chaos of the City's architecture in a logical overall plan. A supreme architect, Dr Christopher Wren, was at hand to supervise this renaissance of the City. Within a week of the disaster he had submitted his ideas for reconstruction. Inspired by the ordered structure of Paris, Wren's designs involved geometric arrangements of avenues radiating towards central and circular meeting points. His plan was characteristic of the ordered, mathematical mind that had made him Professor of Astronomy at Oxford before he turned his hand to architecture at the age of thirty four.

What Wren did not allow for in his plan was the illogical and obstinate cussedness of the Londoner. An overall plan meant pooling the private property of the City and re-distributing it later. But the Londoner was not going to part with his property, even when his freehold was nothing more than a pile of ashes. Days after the Fire, the City began to rise again; but not to Wren's plan, nor to anybody else's. Each householder replaced his property in his own way, without consideration of what was going on next door. The new London became a reconstruction of the old one, a patchwork of unrelated and idiosyncratic units.

The authorities did try, unsuccessfully, to impose certain restrictions upon the freelance developers of the City after the Fire. Houses were to be built of brick or stone, and not with the timber framework that had proved so amenable to fire. It is ironic, but characteristic of London, that buildings which flouted this rule have turned out to be particularly long-lasting. Not a single brick or stone house built immediately after the Fire has survived. But several timber-framed buildings, dating soon after the Fire, still stand. They include the Hoop and Grapes pub in Aldgate High Street, 41-42 Cloth Fair, Smithfield, and 2-3 Middle Temple Lane.

Wren was allowed to re-plan the City's churches in his own way. Even if the City's ground-plan did not conform with his ideas, he was to make its sky-line entirely his own. In addition to St Paul's Cathedral, Wren rebuilt no fewer than 51 of the City's churches as well as three new churches outside the City area. Every Wren church solved new problems in different ways. Paradoxically the variety and invention of Wren's churches was consistent with the unimposed structure of the City's street plan. The diversity of his church spires, towers and domes is rather an apt reflection of the irregularity of the streets that they surmount.

The nearest that London ever got to a grandiose street plan was John Nash's never-finished work of 1813-26 for the Prince Regent, later George IV. Nash built a palace for the Prince, called Carlton House, and re-designed the adjacent park of St James's. Two miles

101 The terraces by John Nash in Regent's Park, commissioned by the Prince Regent and built between 1821 and 1826 were part of the grandest piece of town planning that London has seen. From these terraces a road swept southwards, via Regent Street to St James's Park. The scheme was never completed, and some of Nash's work has since been destroyed. But these "country mansions" survive to show us how London might have been. *Sussex Place, Regent's Park, NW1*

away he landscaped a second park, named Regent's after his patron, and laid out villas and terraces with facades like country mansions. Next, the two parks were linked by a Royal route, lined with elegantly-fronted houses. From St James's Park, Nash's road was cut through to Piccadilly Circus. Here it swept into the gentle curve of the Quadrant of Regent Street, where Nash designed a grand colonnade of shops. The road passed straight up to Langham Place and on to Regent's Park.

Nash's magnificent achievement was soon broken up. The Prince Regent got bored with Carlton House, the centrepiece of the whole project, and had it demolished in 1829. Before he died in 1835, Nash was to suffer the humiliation of seeing the columns from his Royal palace built into the facade of the National Gallery for the sake of economy. The shopkeepers in the Regent Street Quadrant felt that their shops were too much hidden behind Nash's colonnade and it was ripped out in 1848. By 1923 the whole of Nash's Regent Street had been rebuilt. Disrespect was shown for other Nash works too. Marble Arch was his design for the main gateway to Buckingham Palace. It only served this purpose for 23 years before, in 1851, it was moved to the north-east corner of Hyde Park. There it stands still, functionless on a traffic island, known better by name than as a landmark. Buckingham Palace itself, which Nash remodelled in 1824, has been subsequently re-faced; the familiar front, facing the Mall, is not Nash's work but dates from 1912.

One construction by John Nash that has proved surprisingly durable was a tent that he designed for the victory celebrations in St James's Park after the defeat of Napoleon at Waterloo. The tent survives still, sandwiched between an outer sheath of lead, and an inner protective panelling. It is called the Rotunda and serves as the Artillery Museum on Woolwich Common.

Many of London's most familiar buildings are hybrids of different architectural styles, just as the streets themselves are mongrels made up of buildings with diverse pedigrees. Consider the Tower of London. Parts of the Tower are built over the Roman walls of the second century AD. William I's Norman fortress, the White Tower, was completed in 1097, although the turret caps are fourteenth century and the windows eighteenth. Inside, the Chapel of St John is the original Norman structure. Edward I built the Byward Tower. The Queen's House is Tudor and dates from 1540. The army barracks in the Tower, looking medieval in their monumentality, are Victorian, built in 1845.

Some complex London buildings, like Westminster Abbey, are accumulations of architecture from many different periods; but the picture is made even more confusing by the imitation of early styles of architecture in the later periods. The chancel and the beginning of the nave of the Abbey were finished by 1269. After that, building stopped for over a hundred years. But when work resumed and the body of the nave was completed between 1375 and 1500 it was continued in the earlier style which was, by then, quite out of date. The familiar twin towers over the west front of the Abbey do not look out of place in their Gothic context but they were later additions, put up in 1735–40 by Nicholas Hawksmoor. Much of the exterior stonework of the Abbey was replaced in a nineteenth century restoration – thus there is a superficial association between the truly Gothic structure of the Abbey and the Victorian Gothic-revival architecture of the nearby Houses of Parliament.

If there is any one architectural feature that is particular to London it is the London Square. The idea was imported from Italy, but the Square was to become a London institution, more enclosed and private than its continental prototypes. Inigo Jones had travelled in Italy in 1613–14 and in the 1630s he laid out the first of London's squares. This was in Covent Garden and was bordered on the west side by Jones' St Paul's Church. With the Englishman's characteristic confusion over foreign languages, the word "piazza" was used to describe Inigo Jones' arcades around the borders of his square, and not, as in Italy, for the square itself. Bloomsbury Square, which dates from 1665 was the first open space actually to be called a "Square."

102∧

102 A typically elegant London house, and one that people pass every day without noticing anything special. But look again. The windows are painted voids; behind this tree there is a door that does not open. The house is nothing more than a facade, backing onto a line of the Metropolitan Railway.
Leinster Gardens, Bayswater, W2

103 Between 1691 and 1851 an iniquitous tax was levied on householders. They were charged according to the number of windows on their dwellings. Many people saved tax by blocking up some of their windows and usually spoilt the look of their houses in the process. Soon after World War II, a firm of architects, bored with their view onto a bricked-up window, commissioned the painter Brian Thomas to open it up with a cosy domestic scene.
Cloth Court, Cloth Fair, Smithfield, EC1   103＞

104 An unusual late nineteenth century facade that has a glazed ceramic surface with embellishments of eagles, grotesque heads and cherubs.
Maddox St, Mayfair, W1

105 Keats' house in Hampstead. Here, in the spring of 1819, a nightingale built her nest. And here, beneath a plum tree the poet sat for two or three hours and wrote the great ode that predicts his own decline but celebrates the immortality of the bird. Two years later, Keats was dead. But nightingales sing in Hampstead still.
Keat's Grove, Hampstead, NW3

104 >

In Smith Square, Westminster, stands a Church with an unusual design that has earned it the nick-name "Queen Anne's footstool." St John's, Smith Square, was built by Thomas Archer in 1713-28 and embellished with identical stone towers at each of its four corners. Nineteenth century wags, who objected to the baroque fantasy of the decoration, made up the story that the architect had consulted Queen Anne about the design of the Church, and that she had kicked her ornate footstool upside down and replied "Build it like that."

Some of the strangest juxtapositions of architectural styles in London's streets and squares are due to the obstinacy of the Londoner who refuses to be budged from his own little plot in the name of progress, commerce or anything else. Recently there was a massive redevelopment off St Botolph's Churchyard in Bishopsgate. A huge office block was being constructed and the site had been cleared, with the exception of one tiny property, an eccentric Victorian folly, which had been built in oriental tiles as a Turkish bath, but which now functions as a restaurant. The owner would not be moved. Compensation was refused. Finally the development had to go ahead with the design adjusted so that the vast office building would fit snugly around the little Turkish bath restaurant.

A facade in the Mile End Road in East London suggests another battle between the little man and big business. At first sight there is nothing very unusual about Wickham's department store. The architecture is grandiose, as befits a prosperous store, and the long facade is decorated with classical columns and a baroque tower. The odd thing about it is that the shop-front is incomplete. In the middle of this grandiose facade, there is a gap, and the height drops down to a modest little building of an earlier date, that houses a small jewellery shop called Spiegelhalter Bros. On the other side of this little architectural hiccough the heavy facade of the department store resumes its stately progress down the street. The public face of London sometimes puts on a very human expression.

105 ∧

107 ∧

108 ∨

106 ∨

106 The courtyard of the Apothecaries'
Hall dates from 1669-71. The Society of
Apothecaries is the pharmacists' main
examining body.
Blackfriars Lane, EC4

107 Cab-drivers' shelter, built to give
Hansom cab drivers refuge from the cold,
before the days of the motor taxi.
Kensington Park Rd, Notting Hill, W11

108 This glorious gothic folly functions
only as a tool shed.
Lincoln's Inn, Holborn, WC2

Entrances and exits

The Beatles used to have a shop in Baker Street, suitably named Apple Corps, where the door handle was carved in the form of an open hand, held outwards. To open the door one grasped the hand in a warm handshake and nothing could have created a more friendly feeling as one entered the shop.

A few shops have welcoming but disconcerting doors that have no handles; they simply slide open as the customer approaches. Goodes, the china shop in South Audley Street, had a mechanical door-opening device long before the electric eye gadget was invented. As soon as he puts foot on the step, the customer sets the hospitable apparatus into motion.

Doors are for keeping-out as well as for letting-in. In a small alleyway called Lansdowne Row, off Berkeley Street, there is an impediment that can hardly be called a door, a swinging metal bar put there in the eighteenth century after a highwayman escaped down this alley, to block the route.

The front door is a boundary between the public and the private world. Its mood and style suggest whether it opens into an interior of dignity or humour, elegance or shabbiness. It can be friendly or aloof, rich or poor, artistic or vulgar, like the inhabitants within. Elegant door furniture gives a distinction to an entrance. The status of a Harley Street doctor can be assessed by the illegibility of his brass nameplate. Long-established ones are worn smooth by daily polishing.

109 ∧   113 ∨   110 ∧   114 ∨   111 ∧   115 ∨

109 The work of Robert Adam, this is the perfect Georgian doorway.
Mansfield St, Marylebone, W1.

110 One of the loveliest doors in the best-preserved 18th century street in London. Dating from about 1704, an outstanding feature is the intricately carved wooden canopy.
Queen Anne's Gate, Westminster, SW1

111 An imposing door for the medical consultants who practise here.
Upper Wimpole St, Marylebone, W1

112 The classical grandeur of the porch is a late Victorian feature, but the style of the stained glass work in the door dates it to around 1912.
Camberwell (now demolished)

113 The Society of Apothecaries entrance. The horns of both unicorn and rhinoceros were supposed to have medicinal qualities.
Blackfrairs Lane, EC4

114 The cut-away circle of the door, echoed in the arch, are a mark of Christopher Wren's originality. He built this church in 1680.
St Mary-le-Bow Church, Cheapside, EC2

115 A shop door of the 1860's. The sign around the door gives promises of craftsmanship and quality within.
Smith's umbrella shop, New Oxford St, WC1

116 A restaurant door of the 1930's.
Carter Lane, Blackfriars, EC4

117 A door with solid middle-class virtues.
Fulham Palace Road, SW6

118 A classic of *art deco* of the 1930s the Hoover building, characterized by this splendid door, owes something to ancient Egyptian style.
Hoover Ltd, Perivale, Middlesex

116∨   112∧   117∨   118∨

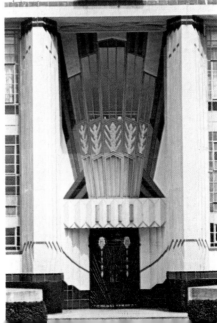

Door furniture

119 An elegant number sign for a London house made with Portuguese tiles.
5 Ladbroke Terrace, W11

120 A bootscraper in Belgravia decorated with cat motifs.
27 Wilton Place SW1

121 *2 Chesterfield Hill, Mayfair, W1*

122 A delicate piece of craftsmanship, this house number has been cut out of sheet metal by hand. Judging by the design, it dates from about 1900.
Orme Square, Bayswater, W2

119∧

120∧   121∨

122∨

123 ∧

124 ∧

126 ∧

125 ∨

127 ∨

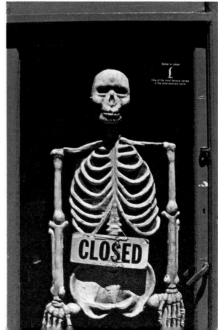

128 ∨

123 Swirling *art nouveau* at a famous pub.
The Salisbury, St Martin's Lane, WC2

124 Decades of daily polishing have left a green stain on the stonework.
8 Eaton Gate, Belgravia, SW1

125 *Lower Grosvenor Place, SW1*

126 *6 Laurence Pountney Hill, City, EC4*

127 Separate bells and separate entrances for "Visitors" and "Servants."
Bayswater Rd, W2 (now removed)

128 There is no disputing that this shop is closed.
The Theatre Zoo, New Row, Covent Garden, WC2

The tradesmen

Around the world the phrase "London Best" is used to describe the supreme product of the gun-maker's craft. Built into the phrase is the assumption that all the best guns are made in London, which is a fact that knowledgeable sportsmen of any nationality will readily confirm. "Savile Row" says much more than the name of a short street in Mayfair. It has come to mean the highest standards in tailoring.

Gun-making and tailoring are only two of the many craft trades that have reached a peak of excellence in London. The Capital's silversmiths, saddle makers, bell founders, violin makers and bookbinders have world-wide reputations. London's sword makers, gold thread embroiderers, furniture makers and restorers, and carpet weavers export their products widely. And the world's wealthy come to London to have their shoes and hats hand-made by experts who have the accumulated skills of many generations of craftsmen behind them.

In the Middle Ages the tradesmen of London could all be found inside the walls of the City. Within this relatively small area they tended to separate into little enclaves of specialists. The basketmakers were in one street, the ropemakers in the next street and so on. Although workshops are now scattered over the vast area of Greater London there are still certain districts with concentrations of craftsmen of a particular trade. Shoreditch is a centre for furniture. Savile Row, Mayfair and Soho are brimful of tailors' work rooms. In Clerkenwell one finds every kind of specialist within the clockmaking and silversmith's trades. This kind of arrangement has great advantages for the craftsmen themselves. Within such communities the individual craftsmen can call upon their colleagues for services that they cannot supply themselves.

London's tradition of excellence in craftsmanship goes back at least six centuries. Fine hand-work was one of the mainstays of the City's wealth. Goods made by the urban craftsmen could be traded against raw materials from the countryside and against imports from abroad. It was in the City's interests to ensure that standards were kept high, both among the craftsmen manufacturers and among the merchants who bought and sold.

It was in the thirteenth century that fraternities of tradesmen received their first Charters from King Edward I that enabled them to set up as governing bodies for their trades. Broadly there were two types of Trade Guilds or "Companies" as they were called. There were the merchant Companies and there were the craft Companies. By the beginning of the fifteenth century there were over a hundred Companies, administering all the main trades that flourished in London at that time. Even the spectacle makers and the tobacco pipe makers came to be represented by their own Companies.

From the beginning the City Companies operated a "closed shop" for their trades. Nobody was allowed to set up in business in the City unless they had first learnt their trade from an established Master. Seven years was the minimum period of apprenticeship. The Companies had the power to seize and destroy any product that was not up to standard, and a craftsman who was found guilty of shoddy work was expelled both from his Company and from the City.

Members of the City Companies were given the Freedom of the City which meant that they were free to come and go as they pleased. Traders from outside were at a disadvantage since they had to pay tolls on entering the City gates. This was an exclusive but efficient system. The London trades became the pride of England: apprentices from all over England competed for positions in the Capital, and foreign merchants competed for the products of the workshops.

The influence of the City Companies over their trades has, with a few exceptions, declined over the last century. Liverymen have won their place by purchase or heredity rather than by apprenticeship, often not actually practising the trade. Sometimes this has resulted in a parallel decline in the trades themselves. Nevertheless, many of the traditions that were established by the ancient trade guilds survive. Apprenticeship does still maintain continuity and families have followed the same trade for several generations. Standards are kept up, and prices down, by competition between the craftsmen themselves.

Buying and selling has passed through several phases of development, each still represented in London today. The first merchants were packmen, itinerant vendors who travelled from town to town and from street to street with their bundles of merchandise.

129 A Battersea Farrier. In the nineteenth century when most of London's transport was horse-drawn every district had its own farrier. Today there are very few about. Bill Geddes shoes horses for many of the rag and bone traders of South London.

The door to door salesman is their modern equivalent.

Some of these traders chose to settle down and set up stalls in street fairs and markets – while still mobile they could stock a much wider range of goods than could be carried in a pack. Street markets are a popular feature of London life, especially for fresh fruit and vegetables, while some have become world famous for antiques and other specialities.

But the street stall is exposed to the weather: stock can be damaged, there is little comfort for the stallholder and it is a nuisance to have to clear the stall at night. The next stage was for the merchant to move indoors. The downstairs rooms of his home were turned into a shop while the shopkeeper and his family continued to live upstairs. This arrangement continues in some small local shops, particularly grocers and newsagents.

Now the shopkeeper had to advertise his presence and attract people to his premises. A hanging sign was a necessity and a show of products in his window was desirable. Soon shop windows were enlarged to increase the area of display. Before the early nineteenth century only small panes of glass could be made but the bow window enabled large windows to be made with small pieces. Hanging signs have now largely disappeared – customers are attracted by the bold name signs above the shopfront, but the development of plate glass has allowed window displays to be enlarged almost without limit.

By opening a shop away from home the merchant created new advantages. The shop could be sited close to other similar premises so that together they formed an attractive shopping centre. Also, if accommodation was not needed above the shop, the extra rooms could be used as an extension of the trading area. London's elegant eighteenth century shops in St James's owe their existence to these factors. Enterprising shopkeepers came here to be near the Court which had moved to St James's Palace after the Palace at Whitehall had been burnt down in 1698. Today this district and nearby, fashionable Bond Street are still enhanced by the presence of a number of distinguished firms. Lock's made the hat that Nelson wore at Trafalgar. Hatchard's sold books to Byron, Macaulay and Thackeray. Berry Brothers and Rudd, the wine merchants, started business as grocers; this explains the origin of the huge pair of scales on which, since 1765, their customers have enjoyed weighing themselves. Fortnum and Mason despatched food parcels to Florence Nightingale in the Crimea and to H. M. Stanley when he was setting out to find Dr Livingstone in Africa. A later arrival to St James's was John Lobb, the bootmaker, from whom the Duke of Wellington ordered the prototype of a functional high leather boot, little realizing that, translated into rubber, it would make his name a household word.

130 Restoration at St Paul's Cathedral. Kenneth Gardner is an architectural sculptor, specialising in carving the stone decorations that embellish London's classical Churches. His father and his grandfather did the same before him. Here he is re-recarving one of Caius Cibber's works, the original of which has eroded.

Once shops had been grouped together in shopping centres it was only a matter of time before all the different services came to be housed under one roof. It was during the nineteenth century that most of London's great department stores were opened by successful drapers and grocers who wished to expand their businesses. The best kind of Department store remains today like a collection of small shops with the barriers between them taken down. But the sheer size of the Department stores allows them to do a phenominal trade. During the spring sales Selfridges in Oxford Street can expect some 150,000 people to pass through the shop in a single day.

The idea of self-service shopping reached England from America in the early 1950's. Since then it has revolutionized the architecture of the High Streets and changed the nation's shopping habits. In London a large number of small family businesses have closed down, their trade usurped by the large supermarkets and multiple stores. Large self-service stores can keep prices down, because of their high turnover and their relatively small number of staff.

131 Stained glass painter. Working on one of the largest expanses of stained glass that has been made this century, the great rose window of Lancing College Chapel, Bill Smith of Goddard & Gibbs Studios paints details onto a small glass fragment. The black and white design is the "cartoon", which serves as a blueprint for the whole window.

132 Approaching his eighties, Mr Ogilvie is one of the last men in London to make brooms by hand. He ties the bristles together with hemp and dips the knot into a pan of hot pitch, which, when cool, fixes it permanently. It takes him twenty minutes to make a broom.

133 A cooper's workshop. Coopering or barrel-making is one of the most ancient craft trades, but one that is disappearing rapidly. Brewers are using metal casks and wine firms are turning to fibreglass. Tom Wood is the cooper at Young's Brewery in Wandsworth, a firm that respects its customers' taste for beer "from the wood."

131∧   **132**∧   **133**∨

The bell foundry

In the year 1593 a bell founder named Robert Mot of Whitechapel re-cast one of the bells of Westminster Abbey. Fifteen years later he re-cast another. And in the course of 378 years that have elapsed since then, the six remaining bells of the Abbey have all been re-cast at the same bell foundry in Whitechapel.

A bell is re-cast when it is cracked or out of tune, the metal from the old bell being melted down and used to make the new one. So although Robert Mot's Westminster bells are certainly old, the metal that is in them has rung far older sounds.

Several weeks of preparation are needed before a bell is cast. First a mould has to be made with a hollow in the middle that is the precise shape of the finished bell. The mould is built in two parts, largely by hand, with yellow London clay. When the inner surfaces of the mould have been smoothed down, the two parts are dried and clamped together and then the mould is ready for casting.

The molten bell metal that is poured into the mould has to be just the right temperature; if it is too hot or too cold the finished bell might crack. After casting, the metal is allowed to cool in the mould for up to eight days. Then the mould is chipped off, the bell is cleaned and ready to be tuned.

Tuning is done by removing metal from the inside of the bell, and the bell is tested both by ear and electronically. The sound of a bell is like a chord made up of several notes; these notes must be in tune with each other. Furthermore each bell must be in tune with the other bells that hang with it.

In 1752 the Liberty Bell of America was first cast at the Whitechapel Foundry. It was re-cast in Philadelphia before it was rung to proclaim the Declaration of Independence on July 4th 1776.

Sadly there are no facilities at the Bell Foundry for spectators unless they are the Foundry's clients. The same applies to the craftsmen shown on the adjacent pages, with the exception of the Whitefriars Glass Works, Harrow, where tours can be arranged.

135∨   134∧

136∨

137 ∨

134 Casting a bell. Molten bell metal, which is an alloy of tin and copper, is poured from a crucible into a carefully prepared mould.

135 A still-life at the bell foundry where the Liberty Bell and Big Ben were cast.

136 Tuning a bell. An unusual form of lathe, on which the bell itself is rotated, and metal shaved from the inner surface.

137 Bells in the yard, waiting to be melted down and their metal re-used.

138 Stephen Gottlieb made his first lute because he wanted an instrument to play himself. The growing interest in early music has created a demand for all sorts of instruments. Stephen Gottlieb bases the designs of his lutes on measurements that he takes from old instruments in museums.

139 Making riding breeches is one of the most skilled branches of the tailor's trade. Edward Head started as an apprentice at fourteen years old. He has now passed eighty, and for sixty years of that time he has made breeches for the same Savile Row firm.

140 Four generations of the Patmore family have worked in the edge-gilding trade. The gold edges of invitation cards and playing cards are put on by hand. The craftsman lays an infinitesimal layer of real gold leaf on each batch of cards, and can gild up to five thousand cards a day.

141 The Whitefriars glass company was already established in 1680. Although the firm has moved from the Embankment to Harrow, the fire of their furnace has never been extinguished. Here a young member of the team blows the first part of a wineglass.
Tudor. Rd, Harrow & Wealdstone

142 The Roman Catholic Church stipulates that candles used in churches must be hand made, and must contain a proportion of beeswax. At Price's candle factory in Battersea a craftsman pours molten wax and builds up the candles gradually with over one hundred thin layers of wax.

143 A bookbinder at Morrells' workshops in Covent Garden sews the sections of a book by hand on a box-wood sewing frame.

140∨    138∧    141∨

139∧ 142∨ 143∨

144 Top hat making. Before the week of Royal Ascot races, Sam Patey and his firm of hatmakers have up to two thousand top hats to repair. Patey's is the only firm in London making hard hats. In addition to silk and grey top hats they make mortar boards, Beefeaters' bonnets, Chelsea Pensioners' three-cornered hats, and riding caps.

145 A collection of hatmakers' tools, bought in 1924 and used every day since then.

144∧   145∨   146∧   147∨

146 One of London's supreme craftsmen, H. L. Pound, maker of edge tools for sculptors and stone carvers. Henry Moore and Barbara Hepworth have used his tools. The lettering on the Cenotaph was cut with tools from his forge, and his mastery is acknowledged by the carvers of Oberammagau in Germany. Now over eighty, Harold Pound has no apprentice to carry on his trade.

147 Copperplate engraving. Stan Apsey of Clerkenwell carries on his father's business, engraving the copper plates from which invitation cards and letterheads will be printed. Everything has to be drawn in reverse.

148 A young engraver reflected in his work, a silver dish on which he is engraving an inscription. His firm, in Hackney is one of London's largest although it only employs seven men. Engravers, like other skilled craftsmen, tend to work alone or in very small businesses.

149 *Barter St, Bloomsbury, WC1*

150 *Curzon St, Mayfair, W1*

151 *Walmer Rd, Notting Hill, W11 (closed)*

152 *Brewer St, Soho, W1 (moved)*

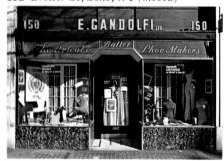

153 *Marylebone Rd, NW1*

A kaleidoscope of shopfronts
Some of London's long-established shop premises.

149 Andrew Block has been in the book trade since 1911.

154 Founded in 1830, James Smith & Son have occupied the present premises, Hazlewood House, since 1857. Their hanging sign appears on page 20 and their shop door on page 60.

155 Lord Nelson used to go to Locks of St

James's to buy his cocked hats. At this shop the bowler hat originated. Here the bowler hat is still called the "Coke" in honour of the customer that first ordered the style.

161 There are several places in London where the traditional pottery jar sign, denoting an oil and colour merchant, is built into the wall above a shop. But it is rare today for a shop that sports this sign to carry on the trade that is represented by the sign.

154 *New Oxford St, Holborn, WC1*

155 *St James's St, SW1*

156 *Warren St, Fitzroy Square, W1*

157 *New Bond St, Mayfair, W1*

158 *Whitechapel Rd, E1*

159 *Westbourne Grove, Notting Hill, W11*

160 *Earlham St, Covent Garden, WC2*

161 *Godfrey St, Chelsea, SW3*

162∧

163∨ 164∧

165∨

166∨

Street trade and entertainment

162 An escapologist draws the crowds at the Saturday Market at Portobello Road. First he invites any man in the audience to bind him. "Women are barred; one woman tied me up forty five years ago and I've been tied up ever since." After the show he takes a collection and pronounces a solemn curse on anyone who does not pay up. *Portobello Rd, W11*

163 The suitcase is a reminder that escapology is an itinerant profession. *Tower Hill, EC3*

164 A busker at the Sunday market at Bethnal Green performs on a homemade instrument, a one stringed mandolin played with a violin bow. The instrument beside him is made from an old kettle.

165 Pets are sold at Bethnal Green Market.

166 A street artist outside the National Portrait Gallery.

STREET MARKETS

Some of London's most interesting outdoor markets; listed according to their speciality but many are general markets as well.

ARTS AND CRAFTS
Bayswater Rd, W2. Paintings on the railings of Hyde Park. *Sundays*
Hampstead Open Air Art Exhibition, Heath St, NW3. *Summer weekends only*

ANTIQUES
Bermondsey Market, Tower Bridge Rd, SE1. The dealers' own market; bargains in the early hours. *Fridays, 5.0 am–9.0 am.*
Portobello Rd (south end), W11. (At the north end there are stalls selling junk, old clothes etc.) *Saturdays.*
Camden Passage, Islington, N1. *Saturdays.*

BOOKS
Farringdon Rd, Clerkenwell, EC1. *Monday–Saturday*

CLOTHES, SHOES, CHINA, NOVELTIES ETC
Petticoat Lane (Middlesex St), E1. London's most famous market and cockney salesmanship at its best. *Sundays*

COINS, SILVER, ANTIQUE JEWELLERY
Cutler St, E1. (Part of Petticoat Lane market) *Sundays*

FLOWERS
Columbia Rd, Bethnal Gn, E2. *Sundays*
East St, Walworth Rd, SW17. *Sundays*

FOOD
Berwick St, Soho, W1. Fruit and vegetables, good and cheap. Exotic and expensive greengrocery at Rupert St, nearby, only a peach-stone's throw from Piccadilly Circus. *Monday–Saturday*
Shepherd's Bush Market, Uxbridge Rd, W12. West Indian specialities. *Wednesday, Friday, Saturday*
Brick Lane, E2. The centre of Bethnal Green market. Asian specialities. *Sundays* (There are other local fruit and vegetable markets in almost every neighbourhood of London.)

JUNK
Cheshire St, E2 (off Brick Lane). Here the rag-and-bone men sell their week's hoard. *Sundays*
Church St, Edgware Rd, W2. *Monday–Saturday*

PETS
Sclater St, E2 (off Brick Lane). Anything from puppies to pirhana fish. *Sundays*

167 A stall in Sclater Street, part of the Sunday morning market at Bethnal Green.

168 "You pick 'em and I'll pack 'em today. You pick 'em and I'll pack 'em. Not a crack or a chip among them. Come on now, who will be the first to buy?" A street salesman at Petticoat Lane Market gathers a set of china together before tossing the whole lot confidently up in the air, and catching it again as one piece.

167∨

16

The writing on the wall

There are two interesting things about any piece of writing in a public place – what it says and how it is written. There is a tendency for people to become curiously pompous when composing public notices, like the one off Rosebery Avenue which reads "Any person found committing a nuisance on these stairs will be prosecuted." In comparison "Please keep off the grass" is impressive for its economy of language.

The style in which a sign is written is equivalent to the tone of voice in conversation. Depending on its style, a sign can convey authority or passion, impatience or aggression. The work of the signwriter has a strong influence on the urban environment, but it is often at its best when least intrusive. The signwriter is an artist, and his street signs and notices are the canvases upon which he expresses not his own personality, but the messages that he wants to convey. A mere house number can be made to complement the architecture of that house, and a notice can be written in such a way that it mirrors the dignity of its surroundings. The London streets are a gallery of the signwriter's art and, as in the other London art galleries, the show is free.

A wall sign in Bethnal Green (*illustrated below*) is a classic of its kind. The style in which it is written is a perfect reflection of the language that it expresses. TEN SHILLINGS REWARD is a straightforward statement and so the lettering is simple and bold. In the subsequent inscription the verbose language is matched by the flowery calligraphy. To convey authority and dignity every word apart from the pronouns is given a capital initial. The artistic demands of the sign have got the better of the signwriter's spelling. He was running short of space when he reached the word "Committing" and so he compressed the letters and left out the second "t." On the other hand he needed to expand the word "Property" to fill a large gap. The sign can be roughly dated by the low value of the reward offered; it must be pre-1920 and it is very likely Victorian. Finally there is the irony that the sign now protects the wall of a derelict property that has long been scheduled for demolition.

Wall signs can serve as valuable social documents, vividly conjuring up echoes of past times. Until very recently there was a notice in Bury Street near the British Museum announcing a by-law "for the suppression of street cries." It demanded that "No person shall for the purpose of hawking, selling or advertising goods, call or shout in any street so as to cause annoyance to the inhabitants of the neighbourhood." Despite its disapproving tone this notice evokes the lovely old street cries of London's past. It conjures up images of flowersellers and matchbox sellers and ladies with baskets of fruit, singing "Cherry ripe – who will buy my sweet ripe cherries..." before being bundled off by the beadles.

Another piece of social history features in a sign on the wall of a house in Colebrook Row, Islington. Very faded with age, the inscription can only just be deciphered. "Hotel for Women Only," it reads, "9d and 1/6 per night. 4/6 and 6/- per week." In decimal currency these figures represent 4p, 8p, 23p and 30p.

169∨

170∨

169 *Virginia Rd, Bethnal Green, E2*

170 One of the oldest street name signs in London. It is on the south side of the street at the Haymarket end. *Orange St (formerly James St), WC2*

171 A left-handed signwriter. *St Mary at Hill, Billingsgate, EC3*

173∧   174∨

<172   175∨

172 The joy of this notice is that it assumes that you are making a noise already and it is to be found at one of the quietest spots along the riverfront. *Below Fishmongers' Hall, Wharfside, EC4*

173 Bitches only – or would that be open to misinterpretation? *Holland Park, W11*

174 By converting a plain English word, urinal, into French this sign's maker tried to make it sound feminine and genteel. *Tower Bridge Rd, Bermondsey, SE1*

175 *Perkins Rents, Pimlico, SW1*

176 The composer of this curiously inappropriate sign was very *particular* that nobody should park in front of it. He wanted to be *particularly* emphatic about this. But he actually manages to reduce the emphasis, for "not particularly" means "not much." Foreign visitors and immigrants must be constantly baffled by such subtleties of the English language. *Westbourne Grove, W2*

176∨

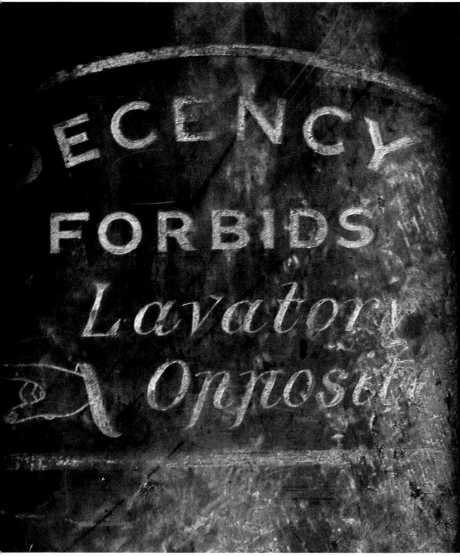

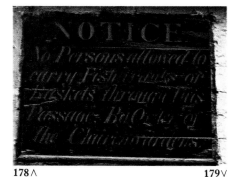

178 ∧

179 ∨

177 ∧

180 ∨

177 Decency forbids. A gem of Victorian euphemism. This sign appears in a gloomy alley in Bayswater and its veiled message invites gentlemen to resist the temptation to urinate against the wall.
Alley off Bayswater Rd, W2, just east of Queensway

178 A curious juxtaposition and calculated to give rise to bad language – Churchwardens giving instructions to fish porters.
St Mary at Hill, Billingsgate, EC3

179 Discrimination for dogs. This notice makes a distinction between dog residents and immigrants and probably infringes some canine race relations act.
Gray's Inn, Gray's Inn Rd, WC1

180 *Lincoln's Inn, Chancery Lane, WC2*

respectively, figures that would need to be multiplied by a hundred to convey the equivalent prices today. This degree of inflation dates the sign to Victorian London, but even then this was no normal Hotel. Why for women only? One assumes that this was some kind of House of correction and the cheap prices, even for the nineteenth century, suggest charity. The sign conveys visions of earnest gentleladies going out to reform the street women and to hustle them away from their territories under the gas lamps into sharp-smelling charitable dormitories.

The sign of the Costermongers' Benevolent Society in Camberwell (*illustrated opposite*) has now been taken down. It carried a haunting reminder of the unfortunate donkeys that used to pull the street market barrows. The costermongers were notoriously hard on their donkeys, and hence the need for a retirement home for the animals to live out their old age in peace. Around the turn of the century there was a donkey fair every afternoon at old Smithfield market. As many as two hundred animals changed hands each day at prices ranging from five shillings to three pounds. Even at these prices a donkey was a status symbol that only the most successful costermonger could afford. The spirit of those times comes to life in the words of the music hall song that Albert Chevalier used to sing in the 1890's:

Last week down our alley came a toff,
Nice old geezer with a nasty cough,
Sees my Missus, takes 'is topper off
In a very gentlemanly way!
"Ma'am," says 'e, "I 'ave some news to tell,
Your rich Uncle Tom of Camberwell
Popped off recent, which it ain't a sell,
Leaving you 'is little Donkey Shay."

CHORUS
"Wot cher!" all the neighbours cried,
"Who're yer goin' to meet, Bill?
Have yer bought the street, Bill?"
Laugh! I thought I should 'ave died,
Knocked 'em in the Old Kent Road!

Some says nasty things about the moke,
One cove thinks 'is leg is really broke,
That's 'is envy, cos we're carriage folk,
Like the toffs as rides in Rotten Row!
Straight! It woke the alley up a bit,
Thought our lodger would 'ave 'ad a fit,
When my Missus, who's a real wit,
Says, "I 'ates a Bus, because it's low!"

When he starts the blessed donkey stops,
'E won't move, so out I quickly 'ops,
Pals start whackin' 'im when down 'e drops,
Someone says 'e wasn't made to go.
Lor, it might have been a four-in-'and,

181 An echo of the past which has now disappeared, and with it the memories of the unfortunate donkeys that pulled the costermongers' market barrows.

182 The Panyer Boy. Erected originally in 1688, the stone relief shows a naked boy sitting on a pannier basket, and marks the spot where bakers' boys used to stand and sell bread from such baskets. The inscription reads "When ye have sought the City Round Yet still this is the highest ground" – a claim that purists would dispute since ground level in Cornhill is two feet higher than here. *Panyer Alley Steps, St Paul's Underground Station, EC4*

183 London's oldest street advertisement. Dated 1680 it advertised Bagnigge House which had a famous tea garden where Nell Gwynne used to come. The Pindar a Wakefielde was a local tavern and there is still a pub of that name nearby. *63 Kings Cross Rd, WC1*

184 The picture is a copy of the painting of a tailor by Moroni in the National Gallery. But what about the inscription BAIS 1866? Actually it stands for nothing more mysterious than "Been At It Since 1866". *The Tailor & Cutter, Gerrard St, Soho, W1*

185 *Westby's sign shop. Hammersmith Rd, W6 (now closed)*

My Old Dutch knows 'ow to do the grand,
First she bows, and then she waves 'er 'and,
Callin' out, "We're goin' for a blow!"

Ev'ry evenin' on the stroke of five
Me and Missus takes a little drive,
You'd say "Wonderful they're still alive,"
If you saw that little donkey go.
I soon showed 'im that 'e'd 'ave to do
Just whatever 'e was wanted to,
Still I shan't forget that rowdy crew,
'Ollerin', "Woa! steady! Neddy woa!"

The "nice old geezer with a nasty cough" might have been suffering from the dreaded disease consumption. In the men's lavatory at Wentworth Street, Whitechapel, a small enamel notice instructs: "Prevention of Consumption: do not spit." Consumption has been called tuberculosis in common speech since early in this century and so the word is evocative in itself. It carries overtones of tragedy and recalls the days before the disease could be checked by medicine when it ran through the population, aggravated by poor housing and under-nourishment and led to painful lingering deaths.

When a lover or a schoolchild carves names on walls we call it vandalism. But when the names were carved long ago they assume a certain historical value. In the Tower of London there are graffiti that are as simply expressed and as crudely cut as any schoolboy's surreptitious efforts with a penknife. But they are eloquent and deeply moving memorials, not only by virtue of their age but also because of the circumstances

181∧   182∨   183∨   184∨

185∨

in which they were made. They are the work of prisoners in the Tower, many of whom were awaiting execution. Cut into the stonework of the Beauchamp Tower is the emblem of the Dudley family. One of the five Dudley brothers was the Earl of Guildford, husband of Lady Jane Grey, who claimed the throne of England and occupied it for ten brief days. The poignant inscription IANE may have been carved by Guildford, or even by Jane's father, the Earl of Suffolk. The three of them were to walk to the executioner's block on the same bleak day in 1554.

In Little Dean's Yard, the central quadrangle of Westminster School, is an elegant stone gateway, built in 1734 and embellished from then onwards with the handsomely engraved names of scholars. Some of them went on to carve distinguished careers for themselves.

Westminster Abbey is the ideal starting point for the student of epitaphs. The Abbey is the national repository for monuments to the Great, although both the Abbey and the memorials suffer from the association. The eye tries to follow the heavenward sweep of the architecture and is brought back to earth by the cramped clutter of monuments at the base. The vast number of tombs and tablets makes it difficult to isolate the gems from the base stones. In the best carved epitaphs the words give the reader a jolt, a shock of recognition of the dead person and a sense of identification with the bereaved. In the east cloister of Westminster Abbey is one such epitaph that is made poignant by its very simplicity:

Jane Lister Dear childe Died Oct 7th 1688

The lettering craftsman's art, like that of the sign writer, is to give to the words that particular form that best expresses their mood. Between about 1620 and 1740 the art seems to have been at a high point, when the carvers had the sophistication to control and adapt their style, without over-elaboration and mannerism.

In the Church of St Dunstan in the West, Fleet Street, is a memorial to Hobson Judkin who is described as an "honest solicitor." It was put up by his grateful clients who may not have intended to imply that honesty was an unusual attribute of a solicitor. In the same church is the epitaph to Alexander Layton, swordsman:

"His thrusts like lightening flew, more skilful Death Parried em all and beat him out of Breath."

A similar sporting metaphor appears on the memorial in Highgate Cemetery to Lillywhite, the cricketer, which shows Death bowling down his wicket.

Humanity and wit are to be found in epitaphs for ordinary people when the words are inspired by affection and grief. Memorials to Great Men are often obsequious and grandiloquent, particularly when they were composed, in advance, by the great men

186 The painter G. F. Watts had the idea of commemorating the heroism of people who died while trying to save the lives of others. In 1880 he gave funds for ceramic tablets to be made and for a shelter to house them in the churchyard of St Botolph-without-Aldersgate. This is just opposite the City's General Post Office; hence its name "Postman's Park." An adjacent plaque commemorates the "clerk who gave up his life for a stranger and foreigner on Ostend Beach." These stories, which pre-date official citations for bravery, are curiously moving in spite of the melodramatic tone of their language.
King Edward St, Smithfield, EC1

187 A beautifully expressed epitaph for a gentleman who "through ye Spotted Vaile of the Small-Pox, rendred a pure & Unspotted Soul to God." The carver of this stone made uninhibited use of Capital letters for emphasis and abbreviations for unimportant words. Evidently he was unsure whether Mr Smith died in 1663 or 4.
Little Cloister, Westminster Abbey, SW1

themselves. The spirit of a famous man may be more easily evoked by going to the place where he lived and by relating his life and achievements to the mundane perspective of his surroundings. London's streets are enriched by a large number of commemorative plaques affixed to houses with distinguished associations. It is a joy to find oneself walking past 180 Ebury Street and imagining the boy Mozart composing his first symphony there, or 22 Frith Street where in 1926 John Logie Baird first demonstrated his invention, television.

The "blue plaques" are a popular London institution although not all of them are blue and not all of them are plaques either. The idea of marking the homes of famous people originated at the Royal Society of Arts in 1864. In 1901 the London County Council (now replaced by the Greater London Council) took over the task of erecting the tablets. The plain blue design with white lettering that is used today was introduced in 1937.

To qualify for a blue plaque a person must have made an important contribution within his field; one hundred years must have elapsed since his birth or twenty five years since his death. Foreign visitors to London are commemorated only when their stay in London was significant in their life and work. In 1976 there were some 365 commemorative tablets maintained by the GLC. In addition there are plaques in the City which are maintained by the City Corporation and a number of tablets erected, with planning permission, by institutions and private individuals.

The blue plaques are outstandingly elegant and although their typography is already forty years old it does not seem dated. The names and symbols of London Transport's underground stations are even older. Designed by Stanley Morison in the early

WILLIAM·GOODRUM

SIGNALMAN·AGED 60

LOST HIS LIFE AT KINGSLAND ROAD BRIDGE

IN SAVING A WORKMAN FROM DEATH UNDER

THE APPROACHING TRAIN FROM KEW

FEBRUARY·28·1880

188 In memory of a cherry pie. On 17th July 1752 two builders were working on scaffolding above Wanstead High Street. A pieman passed below with a tray of tempting pies on his head and the lads bent down and relieved him of one of them. They were caught in the act and fined half a guinea. They carved an inscription which provides a delightfully human record of the event. "In Memory of ye Cherry Pey," it reads "As cost ½ a Guiney ye 17 of July. That day we had good cheer, Hope to do so many a year."
The George Inn, Wanstead, E11

189 Of the three greatest names in English 18th-century furniture, Chippendale, Sheraton and Hepplewhite, only Chippendale is known to have had a hand in the making of some of his pieces. The other two were primarily designers, not makers: their names denote merely a style.
St Martin's Lane, Covent Garden, WC2

186∧ 187∨

In Memory, of Mr THŌ: SMITH, of Elmly-Lovet, in ye Covnty of Worcester, & Bach: of Arts late of Ch:Ch: Oxford. Who throvgh ye Spotted Vaile of ye Small-Pox, rendred a Pvre, & Vnspotted Sovl to God. Expecting, bvt not fearing Death; wᶜʰ ended his dayeˢ, March the 10ᵀᴴ anno Dom 166¾ Ætatis svæ 27·

The Virtues which in his short life were shown, haue equalld been by few, surpassd by none

190∨ 188∧ 189∨

SIR
ALEXANDER
FLEMING
1881-1955
DISCOVERED PENICILLIN
IN THE SECOND STOREY
ROOM ABOVE THIS
PLAQUE

190 In a little room above this modest plaque one of the great moments in the history of medicine took place. The mould that came in through the window from the grimy London street gave rise to a drug that has saved literally millions of lives.
St Mary's Hospital, Praed St, W2

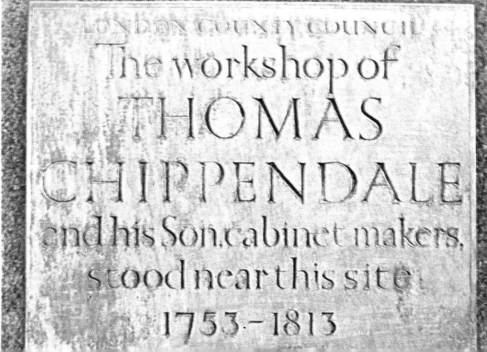

LONDON COUNTY COUNCIL
The workshop of
THOMAS
CHIPPENDALE
and his Son, cabinet makers,
stood near this site
1753 – 1813

1930's, they are as simple, clear and stylish as anything done since.

London's street name signs offer more than good design. London's past can be traced back through her place names and a study of their origins can give intriguing glimpses into history. There is a surprising link between two famous London addresses, Charing Cross and the Elephant and Castle. There are attractive theories that both were named after the well-loved wife of Edward I. Edward's Queen was Eleanor of Castile, and this name could easily have become corrupted in the common speech of an illiterate population to "Elephant and Castle." Queen Eleanor died in 1290 at Harby in Nottinghamshire. Her body was brought to be buried in the Abbey at Westminster, a journey that took thirteen long days. The cortege stopped each night at the roadside. The following year Edward marked the resting places with magnificent stone crosses. The last halt had been at a small hamlet only a mile from the Abbey. Here the last of the crosses commemorating the dear Queen, *"la chere reigne,"* gave to the place its name, Charing Cross.

The original Eleanor Cross was destroyed by a mob, egged on by Puritan preachers, in 1643, but in 1865 a Victorian reconstruction was placed at a new site in the Strand, in front of Charing Cross Station. Another theory about the word "Charing" gives it an earlier, Anglo-Saxon origin; it is here that the river makes a "char" or bend.

Predictably the streets around St Pauls Cathedral have ecclesiastical connections but these date back to before Henry VIII's break with Rome. It is conjectured that street names here originated from the progress of solemn processions around the Cathedral precincts. The Lord's Prayer would have been sung in Latin at Paternoster Row. This came to an end as the procession reached Amen Court. Then came the Hail Mary in Ave Maria Lane and the Credo in Creed Lane.

Before the monasteries were stripped of their power and their properties in Henry VIII's time, they were able to give refuge to outlaws, provided that they had not committed treason or crimes against the Church. The Law could not lay hands on a man within the monastic "sanctuary." Broad Sanctuary is still the name of the precinct beside Westminster Abbey and it bears witness of the Abbey's monastic origins.

There is still one sanctuary in London where the police do not go. This is Ely Place, which used to be the precinct of the Bishop of Ely's palace. A commissionaire stands at the entrance to preserve law and order.

When Henry VIII dissolved the monasteries, he gave the Priory of St Mary of Bethlehem to the City of London for use as a lunatic asylum. By the eighteenth century the Bethlehem Hospital, its name corrupted to "Bedlam," had become a hellish place of suffering.

191 Elastic glue was probably some kind of rubber solution; it is not made in this little shop any more, but large firms have made their fortunes on the idea.
Earlham St, Covent Garden WC2

192 Winkles and shrimps every Sunday. This abrupt sign appears to be offering the sacraments of a new religion. In fact it marks the front door of the home of a popular shellfish stall holder. During the week he sells winkles and shrimps from his stall. On a Sunday, knowing that the London addict cannot go for twenty-four hours without a dish of winkles, he dispenses them from home.
Farringdon Road, Clerkenwell, EC1

193 St Martin is the patron saint of saddlers and St Martin's Lane was traditionally the centre of the saddlery trade. This wall sign dates from the turn of the century. The census of 1901 reveals that there were some 4,179 saddlers in London then, compared with a mere handful now.
St Martin's Lane, WC2

194 There are plenty of shop name signs that feature a father "and sons" combination but John Dennis' proud announcement of his eight children is unique, and has become one of the off-beat landmarks of London.
John P. Dennis, Westbourne Grove, Notting Hill, W11

195 This lovely square could still provide subjects for England's greatest landscape painter, but the sun sets now behind a row of houses put up after Turner's time.
Campden Hill Square Garden (North side), Kensington, W8

196 Ellen Keeley: On Hire. The costermongers' market barrows are unique to London. Unique too is the style of lettering that the barrow-makers engrave on the sides and on the wheels of their barrows. Barrows are always hired, never sold. The barrow-maker can instantly recognize his work by his distinctive brand of lettering.
Berwick St Market, Soho, W1

People came to watch the inmates through the bars like animals in a zoo. Hogarth illustrated Bedlam as the final degradation of "The Rake's Progress." The word has become an idiom of everyday language, used to describe any kind of mad chaos. Similarly Carey Street is a metaphor for bankruptcy generally, although its origin is specifically a London one. London's bankrupts were sent to the Court at Carey Street for trial. Likewise, the Clink was a London prison, but the word has entered the language as a slang expression for any prison.

The names of the gates into the walled City of London survive, although the metropolis has long outgrown her walls. Aldgate, Aldersgate, Billingsgate, Bishopsgate, Cripplegate, Dowgate, Ludgate, Moorgate, Newgate: here strangers had to pay tolls before entering the City. After the curfew hour, the City gates were closed but latecomers might be admitted by a subterranean entrance at Cripplegate. The Anglo-Saxon word *crepel* means underground passage.

Milk Street and Bread Street in the City were named after the commodities that were sold there. Ropemaker Street, Threadneedle Street and Cloth Fair tell the story of their ancient connection with the craft trades.

191∧

192∧

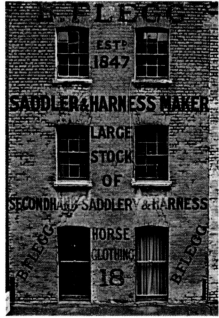

193∧

194∧

195∧

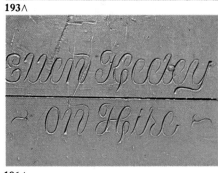

196∧

SOME ADDRESSES OF THE FAMOUS

John Logie Baird (1888–1946) first demonstrated television at 22 Frith St, Soho, W1 in 1926.

Captain Bligh (1754–1817) of *HMS Bounty* lived at 100 Lambeth Rd, SE1.

Canaletto (1697–1768), Venetian painter, lived at 41 Beak St, Soho, W1, in 1746–56.

Sir Winston Churchill (1874–1965) lived at 28 Hyde Park Gate, Kensington, SW7.

Sir Arthur Conan Doyle (1859–1930), creator of Sherlock Holmes, practised as a doctor at 2 Devonshire Place, W1. The fictional detective lived at 221b Baker St. A Post Office employee still replies to letters sent to Holmes at this non-existent address.

John Constable (1776–1837), painter, lived at Well Walk, in NW3 and at 76 Charlotte St, W1, where he died.

Charles Dickens (1812–1870) lived at 48 Doughty St, WC1, between 1837–9 (House open to the public, Mondays–Saturdays).

Sir Edward Elgar (1857–1934), composer, lived at 51 Avonmore Rd, Hammersmith, W14.

Friedrich Engels (1820–1895) lived at 121 Regents Park Rd, NW1 in 1870–94.

Michael Faraday (1791–1867) scientist was apprenticed at 48 Blandford St, W1.

Benjamin Franklin (1706–90), American statesman and scientist, lived at 36 Craven St, WC2.

Sigmund Freud (1856–1939) lived at 20 Maresfield Gns, Hampstead, NW3, in 1938–9.

Mahatma Gandhi (1869–1948) stayed at Kingsley Hall, Powis Rd, E3 in 1931.

George Frederick Handel (1685–1759) composed "The Messiah" at 25 Brook St, Mayfair, W1.

Guglielmo Marconi (1874–1937), pioneer of wireless communication, lived at 71 Hereford Rd, Bayswater, W2, in 1896–7.

Karl Marx (1818–83) lived at 28 Dean St, Soho, W1 in 1851–6.

Piet Mondrian (1872–1944), painter, lived at 60 Parkhill Rd, Hampstead, NW3.

Samuel Morse (1791–1872), American painter and inventor of the Morse code, lived at 141 Cleveland St, W1 in 1812–15.

Wolfgang Amadeus Mozart (1756–91) composed his first symphony at the age of eight, while staying at 180 Ebury St, Victoria, SW1.

Samuel Pepys (1633–1703), diarist, lived at 12 Buckingham St, WC2 in 1679–88.

Vincent van Gogh (1853–90), Dutch painter, lived at 87 Hackford Rd, SW9 in 1873–4.

John Wesley (1703–91), founder of Methodism, lived at 47 City Rd, Finsbury, EC1.

William Wilberforce (1759–1833), campaigner against slavery, died at 44 Cadogan Place, SW1.

Oscar Wilde (1854–1900) lived at 34 Tite St, Chelsea, SW3.

William Butler Yeats (1865–1939) lived at 23 Fitzroy Rd, Primrose Hill, NW1.

The name of Knightrider Street echoes with the clatter of the Knights Templars' horses trotting from the Tower to the jousting tournaments near the Temple. The street is mentioned in documents of 1332.

Piccadilly, one of the main thoroughfares of London was named after an ephemeral clothing accessory of the seventeenth century: the pickadil, a kind of ruff worn at the collar. George Baker was a tailor successful enough to own a large property which, by 1623, was called Piccadilly Hall. He probably sold plenty of pickadils at his shop but the name was unlikely to have been of his choosing. It may well have arisen as a joke, intended to deflate the small tradesman who had come up in the world. But the title stuck and George Baker's house gave the street its name.

Off the Strand there is a unique collection of adjacent streets whose names commemorate the noble gentleman whose palace used to occupy the site. George Villiers, Duke of Buckingham, was a court favourite of Charles I. And George Street, Villiers Street, Duke Street, Of Alley (Now re-named "York Place, formerly Of Alley"), and Buckingham Street are still there to commemorate his memory.

King Edward III put his ceremonial robes of state on

197 Silent protest: more convincing when the grammar is correct. *In Whitehall, SW1*

198 Even London's graffiti are cosmopolitan. Britain's tradition of free speech allows a wide range of political expression, but defacing buildings with slogans of violence is doubly illegal.

197∧   198∨

بیروز باد مبارزه مسلحانه تنهاراه رهائی خلقهای ایران

display at Wardrobe Place. King's Road was the route that Henry VIII and later monarchs took from London to the Palace at Hampton Court. Henry used to hunt in the forest that is now Hyde Park and Rotten Row, the riding track across the Park, was probably *route du roi*. We know that Charles II enjoyed the Flemish game Paille Maille, but the street in St James's was already called Pall Mall before his reign. It was almost certainly called after the game.

Mount Street in Mayfair was the site of Oliver's Mount, a Parliamentary fortification at the time of the Civil War. Mayfair itself was named after an annual fair held during the first two weeks of May, between 1688 and 1760, on what was then the meadows outside London. The Haymarket was held on three days a week for the sale of hay and straw.

Modern street names tend to be less interesting than older ones, largely because literacy has wiped out the opportunities for words to become corrupted. But graffiti can still make a positive contribution. The bleak walls of the railway approach to Paddington have an inscription that is as cheering as a rose on a prison wall. "Far away is close at hand," it reads, "in images of elsewhere."

199 Standing up for his principles. Always cheerful, always courteous, this gentleman bicycles into central London from Northolt in Middlesex and walks up and down Oxford Street for up to eight hours a day with his passionate placard. Millions of people must have read his message; few can have digested it. *Usually near Oxford Circus, W1*

199>

London's countryside

Baedeker's Guides to London in the early 1900's used to warn visitors travelling by train to Brighton from Victoria Station that "Open countryside is not reached until you have passed Clapham." London's choking collar of suburbs has spread so much in the intervening years that open countryside cannot now be seen for the first thirty miles of the journey.

The country-lover in London need never feel hemmed-in. Even in the centre he can enjoy the open spaces that have been preserved in the heart of the Capital. The parks and gardens, heaths and commons have a wealth of wild life that can take the natural history specialist by surprise.

When a zoological survey was made of the insects that were to be found in the gardens of Buckingham Palace several hundred different species were recorded. Among them there was one small moth that was totally new to Britain. It was speculated that it had been imported on the clothes of a foreign dignitary visiting the Queen and had settled when it found the royal surroundings comfortable.

The Black Redstart is a bird that is not uncommon in Europe, but before the 1920's it was a rare visitor to Britain. About that time it first bred there, and one of the main breeding colonies was in Central London. For years this pretty little bird was hardly noticed although thousands of people must have seen it. During World War II London's Black Redstart colony grew from strength to strength. One pair nested on Westminster Abbey. The bomb-sites of the City and the East End became a perfect habitat for the bird, the broken walls and rubble making ideal nesting sites. In springtime the male birds could be heard singing lustily above the roar of the City traffic.

Large numbers of migrant birds pass across London each spring on their way to the breeding grounds. Often they are to be seen in greater concentrations in London than elsewhere because of the relatively limited number of places where they can settle. In the right season the woodlands of Regents Park, Greenwich Park and Wimbledon Common are good places to see the Spotted Flycatcher, Whitethroat, Willow Warbler, Chiff-Chaff and the Blackcap.

A famous lyric celebrates the nightingale that sang in Berkeley Square, and this is not just a romantic fantasy. One of the most moving tape-recordings of bird song was made during World War II in the middle of the London Blitz. A nightingale can be heard singing heartily and with total disregard for the background accompaniment of exploding bombs.

Birds of prey are not uncommon. Owls frequently disturb the sleep of Kensington residents. Kestrels can be seen hawking across the sheer cliff landscape of the high-rise buildings of London.

Dense human populations can be an asset to certain kinds of wild life. Pigeons, sparrows and starlings are obvious examples that have adapted so well to the urban habitat that they have become a pest. Large human settlements require the services of reservoirs, sewage farms and refuse tips, and all these attract a wealth of bird life. Practically every species of duck, grebe or diver that visits Britain has been recorded on

200, 201 Seasonal variations in a London park, autumn (*right*) and winter (*left*). The small area of woodland in Holland Park is an ideal habitat for wild birds that include the Greater Spotted Woodpecker, the Tawny Owl and the Tree Creeper. Exotic birds such as peacocks and flamingoes can be seen here too, looking as strange and bedraggled in winter as the palm trees under their sprinkling of snow.
Holland Park, Kensington, W8

London's reservoirs. Barn Elms Reservoir, SW13 is especially good for waders and wildfowl. Walthamstow Reservoir, N17 is a nesting site of the Heron and the Great Crested Grebe; both sites can be visited on permits available from the Metropolitan Water Board, Rosebery Avenue, EC1.

Mammals cannot travel across the urban landscape so easily as birds, but London's open spaces have mammal populations that were either stranded there originally or subsequently introduced. Badgers and foxes, stoats and rabbits are found on Hampstead Heath. The foxes and badgers supplement their natural diets with forays to the dustbins of residents in the streets nearby. Some stray further afield. One fox was hit by a car at Blackfriars Bridge which is miles from any likely habitat. In Richmond there are herds of Red Deer and Fallow Deer as there have been since Charles I enclosed the Park for a royal hunting ground.

London has been described as a collection of villages, and indeed London has grown, amoeba-like, by absorbing the surrounding communities. The London districts of Hampstead, Highgate, Dulwich, Camberwell, Kensington and Chelsea, to name only a few, were ancient settlements long before they were engulfed by London, and many of them retain their intimate village scale and atmosphere.

Traces of the village industries of past years are still to be found in surprising places. There are windmills at Brixton, Wimbledon and Upminster. The latter is the largest complete smockmill in the Eastern Counties and was used for grinding flour up to the first World War. Tobacco leaves used to be ground into snuff at a mill that still exists on the River Wandle at Morden. At Bromley-by-Bow there is a mill that harnessed the power of the tides on the River Lea.

Riding a horse is regarded as a country pursuit, illogically perhaps, since until a century ago the horse was the chief mode of urban transport. Within London

202∨

202 Springtime in Kensington Gardens, the Albert Memorial beyond. The figure of Prince Albert, with the catalogue of the Great Exhibition of 1851 in his hand, was unveiled by Queen Victoria in 1872.

203 Alive with gnomes, hobgoblins and plaster rabbits, this much-loved family garden in a Camberwell suburb transcends the innate ghastliness of such objects and becomes a thing of beauty. Each dwarf, each plant, each decorative urn is tended so affectionately that a gardening cliche is turned into an original work of art. The windmill gives a clue to the gardener's country of origin and the name of his house, "The Hook of Holland" gives the game away.
Knatchbull Rd, Camberwell, SE5

203>

204 Enjoying the shade of a Mulberry tree on a sultry summer afternoon.
Holland Park, Kensington, W8

205 This kiln fired flower pots and drain pipes for nineteenth century London. The name of a nearby street, Hippodrome Mews, recalls a horse track that once occupied the site.
Pottery Lane, Notting Hill, W11

206 A windmill of 1816, just beside Brixton prison.
Off Blenheim Gardens, Brixton, SW2

<204   205∧   206∨

one can still find a greater concentration of horses and horse-drawn vehicles than in any comparable area of the provinces. The horse is indispensible to London's pageantry. The Household Cavalry and the King's Troop of the Royal Horse Artillery are mounted regiments, barracked and stabled in central London. The Metropolitan Police keep a number of horses, largely for ceremonial duties. The "totter" or rag and bone man with his shaggy horse and cart is a familiar London sight, and the breweries keep teams of massive carthorses to pull their drays.

Hyde Park and Regent's Park formed part of the forest preserved by Henry VIII for hunting wild boar. Today the parks provide every Londoner with a breath of countryside on his doorstep. There are no fewer than eighty parks within seven miles of Piccadilly, providing landscapes which, if not actually rural, are laid out according to the human idea of what rural beauty should be. Here is a comfortable countryside, with none of the impedimenta of the true country, such as stinging nettles and barbed wire, brambles and quagmires. Here the Londoner can indulge his atavistic desire for the outdoor life without getting his feet dirty. Here he can ride his horse, exercise his dog, run a mile, sunbathe, fly a kite, skate, watch birds, swim in the nude (not everywhere; only on Wimbledon Common), play golf, sail a boat and catch butterflies, if he likes; but not all at once.

207 Early morning exercise for a trooper of the Household Cavalry and his horses beside the serpentine, in Hyde Park. The Serpentine is formed by the River Westbourne, which runs underground to join the Thames at Chelsea. At Sloane Square it meets the Underground railway, and flows through a square iron conduit an uncomfortable fifteen feet *above* the platform.

207∨

Fresh milk and meat

The English take it for granted but visitors find it astonishing that nearly every City dweller in the land can have fresh milk delivered to his doorstep if he wants it. Before the days of bulk transport and refrigeration a daily delivery of fresh milk throughout London was an even more extraordinary achievement.

As transportation has improved over the years the dairy pastures have receded further from Central London. Until the 1870's cows were still grazing in the meadows of Kensington. From this distance delivery by horse and cart to the central districts was not difficult. The problem, though, was to provide enough milk from these outlying farms. For many dairymen the solution was to keep their own cows on the premises, even in built-up neighbourhoods.

Dairymen used to buy cows that had recently calved and kept them in back yards and even in basements for a few months until their milk ran dry. The cows were then returned to their farms and exchanged for new milkers.

Farmers from Wales, and particularly those from Cardiganshire, were the best suppliers of milking cows to London. Many Welsh dairy farmers came to settle in the capital and to this day it is noticeable that the small dairy shops of London often carry Welsh names, like Davies, Owen, Evans and Jones, and are still run by Welsh families.

Before deep freezers were heard of, supplies of fresh meat were obtained by the simple expedient of keeping the livestock alive until its meat was needed. Drovers brought their beasts into the heart of the City and the central meat market, Smithfield, stands on the site of a "Smooth Field" where, livestock auctions used to be held. In 1757 a wide new road, now Marylebone and Euston Roads, was built to make it easier for West Country farmers to drive their sheep and cattle to market.

Some butchers in Central London used to have grazing rights for their flocks and herds in the Royal Parks. During the last World War, when the country was striving to be self-sufficient in food, these rights were revived and herds of sheep were seen again in Hyde Park.

Today many young people are thinking again about self-sufficiency, and are moving back to the land. Even within London this trend is in evidence. Derelict land in the docks area of the East End has been reclaimed and made over to pasture. Goats and chickens are bringing waste land back to life. And in a quiet street in Clapham there is even a house with a cow in the back garden providing fresh milk daily for her owners.

208–212 Murals on a disused dairy. *Stroud Green Rd, Finsbury Pk, N4*

213 The cow's head on the wall denotes the site of an old dairy; cows were kept at the back of the shop until 1914. The sun was probably added later, after the premises became an antique business. *Old Church St, Chelsea, SW3*

214 The model of a cow in the window of a snack bar gives a clue that the shop was once a dairy with cows on the premises. *Chalton St, Somers Town, NW1*

215 Mr Owen of Camberwell is the last of the London dairymen to do his rounds with a hand-cart. He starts early, at 5.00 am to avoid the traffic, and all his customers have their milk by 7.00 am. *Camberwell New Rd, SE5*

208∧

209∨

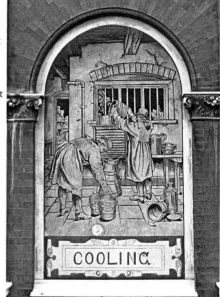

213∨

211∧

BUTTER

212∨

GRAZING

DELIVERY

210∧ 214∨

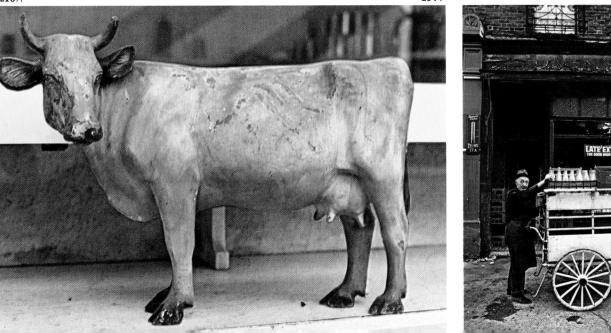

215∨

Gardens and graves

"God Almighty first planted a garden," wrote Francis Bacon, Lord Chancellor of England, "and it is indeed the purest of human pleasures." Bacon's own accomplishments as a gardener can still be seen at Gray's Inn, Holborn. Bacon was Treasurer of Gray's Inn and kept chambers here until his death in 1626. The gardens that he laid out are open from Monday to Friday between 12.45 and 2.15 pm. Here there is one of the finest Catalpa trees in London, said to have been planted by Bacon from seed brought back from America by Sir Walter Raleigh.

Seeds from a London garden were sent to America to establish the first cotton plantations of the South. This was in 1732 and the seeds were supplied by the Chelsea Physic Garden. This garden was maintained by the Apothecaries' Company and it is now administered by the City Parochial Foundation. It still provides herbs for medicinal and teaching purposes, but it is not generally open to the public.

Laid out in 1673 the Chelsea Physic Garden is second only to the Botanic Garden at Oxford as the oldest in Britain. Ironically it was at Oxford, in 1670, that London's own particular tree, the London Plane, was first grown. Two distinct species, the Oriental Plane from the Eastern Mediterranean and the North American Plane were growing side by side, and they hybridized to give the London Plane. It is better suited than either of its progenitors to cold winters and to urban pollution. The plane trees of Berkeley Square have stood up comfortably to both since 1789.

Londoners love to indulge in the purest of human pleasures even if their gardens are no bigger than a window box or a herb tray on a kitchen shelf. Basement dwellers cultivate any corners that the light touches, while high-rise flats, like Babylon, have hanging gardens.

Everybody knows that the English are devoted to their pets. Perhaps it is not surprising then that so many cherished animals are commemorated in London's graveyards. On the edge of Hyde Park at Lancaster Gate there is a dogs' cemetery, founded by the Duke of Cambridge in 1880. And in Cambridge Avenue, Kilburn, is the animals' Cenotaph, a memorial to all the horses, mules and dogs that died on active service in the two World Wars.

216 All day and every day for over two years this lady has set up camp outside the barracks of the Household Cavalry with all her wordly possessions in plastic bags beside her. She is such a fixture that the officers and men raise their caps to her in salute as they ride their horses into the Park for exercise. Her proximity to the senior regiment of the British Army gives her security that she feels she needs.

217 An immortal gardener, this lady of stone seems to be tending her roses still.
Highgate Cemetery, N6

218 Faithful unto death, a dog guards his master's grave.
Highgate Cemetary, N6

<216   217∧   218∨

219 At the
Chelsea Flower
Show, held in the
grounds of the
Royal Hospital.
This is England's
leading
horticultural
exhibition at
which
nurserymen
compete for prizes
awarded by the
Royal
Horticultural
Society and high
fashion jostles
with country
gardeners.
*Royal Hospital,
Chelsea, in May*

220 The
Londoner's street
is his garden. An
enterprising
gardener has
trained a
promising crop of
runner beans up
the railings.
*Ladbroke Grove,
Notting Hill, W11*

221∧

219∧

220∨

221 Up for the day, a visitor to the Royal Horticultural Society's autumn show. *RHS Hall, Vincent Sq, Westminster, SW1*

222 As if fulfilling Macbeth's fear that "Birnam Wood do come to Dunsinane," the Chelsea flower show takes to its legs as soon as the public exhibition is over, and makes its way to the omnibus. The public are allowed to buy the exhibits and they carry them off to their own gardens. *Late May, Royal Hospital, Chelsea, SW3*

223 A Thames water garden: a small but cherished plot on a Chelsea houseboat. *Chelsea Embankment, SW3*

222 ∧   223 ∨

The river

One fine summer morning in 1802 a young man and his sister crossed the river at Westminster on their way by coach to Dover. In her journal the sister recorded:

"Left London between five and six o'clock of the morning outside the Dover coach. A beautiful morning. The City, St Paul's with the river and a multitude of little boats, made a beautiful sight as we crossed Westminster Bridge; the houses were not overhung by their cloud of smoke, and they were spread out endlessly; yet the sun shone so brightly, with such a fierce light, that there was even something like the purity of one of Nature's own grand spectacles."

As the coach travelled to Dover the young man composed his own evocation of the view.

"Earth has not anything to show more fair:
Dull would he be of soul who could pass by
A sight so touching in its majesty:
This City now doth, like a garment, wear
The beauty of the morning: silent, bare,
Ships, towers, domes, theatres and temples lie
Open unto the fields, and to the sky;
All bright and glittering in the smokeless air . . .
. . . The River glideth at his own sweet will:
Dear God! the very houses seem asleep;
And all that mighty heart is lying still!"

The brother and sister who crossed Westminster Bridge were William and Dorothy Wordsworth. Their descriptions conjure up a vivid picture of a pre-industrial London riverside, with its elegant vista of buildings clustered around the central thread of the Thames. The clarity of the light, the purity of the air and the intimacy of the scene is reminiscent of the lagoons and canals of eighteenth century Venice in the paintings of Canaletto. In fact that great Venetian painter came to London, and painted the Thames in just the same light that the Wordsworths saw it. In

1746 Canaletto chose a view of the river from a terrace off Whitehall, only a few hundred yards downstream from Westminster Bridge which was being built at the time. His painting shows a clear panorama of the city, the view of St Paul's and the spires of the Wren churches unobstructed by any impurities in the crisp air. Canaletto's Thames is a clean blue. A pair of stately barges is proceeding upstream, surrounded by a little flotilla of small rowing craft. The Thames is revealed as a great highway, linking the twin cities of London and of Westminster. The barges suggest the river's use as a fashionable centre of pleasure and pageantry. At the same time the water is clearly a barrier, dividing the north and south banks, so that there seem to be two separate and independent Londons.

Only fifty years after the Wordsworths had written

224 Seen from the waterfront at Rotherhithe the sun sets behind St Paul's Cathedral with the modern landmark, the Post Office Tower, some two miles beyond. Tower Bridge is the last of London's bridges before the sea, and one of the most familiar to visitors. Many mistakenly think it is London Bridge, including, at first, the Americans who bought old London Bridge and reassembled it in the Arizona desert.
View from: Cherry Garden, Rotherhithe, SE16

about the view from Westminster Bridge, Charles Dickens described a very different image of the Thames. In 1851 he composed an imaginary conversation with the river itself in *Household Words*:

"'... How very thick the water is hereabouts, Father Thames; and, pray, may I inquire what that black, sluggish stream may be which I see pouring into you from a wide bricked archway, yonder?'

'Oh that's one of my sewers' replied the Father of Rivers ...

'But what are those smaller mouths that send forth strange party-coloured currents to mingle with your waters?'

'That one belongs to a soap boiler – a particular friend of mine; the next to it, is from a slaughter-house, kept by a very estimable friend indeed, who wouldn't allow a particle of the refuse and drainage of his yards to run anywhere else, on any account ... Those other agreeable little outlets ... are from gas-factories, brewhouses, shot-factories, coal-wharfs, cow-houses, tan-pits, gut-spinners, fish-markets, and other cheerful and odoriferous tributaries; while the inky flood yonder which your eyes are now fixed upon is from a very populous grave-yard, which produces so large a quantity of liquid every four-and-twenty hours, that it has to be drained off by regular arrangement, and made to flow into my convenient, all-embracing bosom.'"

Dickens was writing soon after some two hundred thousand private cesspools had been closed, and their input diverted to the main sewers, which opened into the Thames. At high tide the flow of sewage was reversed as the river ran up the pipes. Certainly the stench that had characterized London for centuries was reduced in the streets, but it simply transferred to the Thames. With an unusually hot summer and a low rainfall in 1858, the Year of the Great Stink, the river became an almost undiluted flow of foetid sewage. River traffic ceased and Parliament was adjourned on several days as the smell was intolerable. An engineer named Gurney suggested that the offensive gases could be piped off and burnt, but he was not allowed to demonstrate his device for fear that he would use it to blow up Parliament.

Not long after the Great Stink the river in Central London was made less offensive when huge outflows were built to release London's sewage far downstream in the Thames estuary. Still the pollution was a barrier to any forms of life coming up-river from the sea, and it is only recently that purification plants have become effective. Life is slowly ebbing back into the Thames water. An unexpected sight in Tudor London was Henry VIII's polar bear, allowed out of the Tower on a lead to catch salmon in the Thames. Neither salmon nor polar bears have been re-established in the new waters of the Thames, but there have been some surprising visitors. In 1976 three small crabs were found in West Thurrock power station on the Thames. Called the Chinese Mitten Crab, because of its furry claws, this species is a native of the Fukien province of China. Presumably the crabs, or their ancestors, stowed away in the water ballast tanks of Chinese vessels, and were discharged at the London docks.

London's docks system extends from the Tower of London eastward for twenty-three miles to Gravesend. One of the principal docks was designed in 1800-05 by the architect of Dartmoor prison. Its fortress-like security was intended to protect cargoes from river thieves. Before the docks were built merchant ships moored on the open river and were easy prey for thieves who seemed undeterred by the punishment inflicted if they were caught. Execution Dock at Wapping marks the place where executed pirates were hung in chains until the tide had ebbed and flowed three times, alternately washing and exposing their bodies.

Since World War II trade has become concentrated at down-river docks, like Tilbury, while the docks nearer London have declined. St Katherine's Dock, adjacent to Tower Bridge, closed to shipping in 1969. When it was first built in 1827-28 this dock displaced no fewer than 11,300 people from their homes. Now the magnificent buildings, designed by Thomas Telford, with warehouses that once held commodities like indigo, tallow, mohair, hops and shells, have been turned back into homes again. A yachting marina occupies the basin where once the merchant vessels used to unload. As the river's industry recedes, and domestic and industrial pollution disappears, the Thames is beginning to resume its role as a centre of leisure and entertainment.

The unpolluted Thames seen by Canaletto and Wordsworth was a pleasure centre for Londoners and a highway of State pageantry. The riverside gardens of Vauxhall and Ranelagh were fashionable places of entertainment where Society went to sport itself, to sing and dance, and enjoy bright lights and fireworks. Lord Mayors' processions were waterborn, and so were State funerals, like that of Nelson. These activities came to an end with the Great Stink of the nineteenth century, and with the increasing industrialisation of London's riverside. Industrial architecture turned its back on the river. New bridges made passenger transport on the Thames redundant. For a century or so, the social life of the river, like its water, was dead.

Hitler's bombs blew great gaps in the industrial facades of the Thames. After the war the Festival of Britain of 1951 celebrated the end of the years of austerity. Fittingly the Festival brought a riverside

225∨

225 Generations of Londoners have lost or thrown things into the Thames, and treasure hunters today have the benefit of sophisticated metal detectors. Dredging and building excavations have exposed some of the best finds. Among other things, the Thames mud has surrendered a Roman portrait in bronze of the Emperor Hadrian, and fragments of weapons used by the ancient Britons in Boadicea's time.
Lowtide at Rotherhithe SE16

226 Twenty years ago a boy fishing in the Thames would have been laughed to scorn by his schoolmates. Not so now. Anti-pollution regulations are proving so effective that no fewer than 91 species of fish have been recorded recently within the tidal reaches of the river. This figure includes a sea horse, found at Dagenham, and a 3½ pound rainbow trout. Salmon have not been caught in the Thames since 1833, but now 5,000 salmon fry have been released in the river at Twickenham in an attempt to reintroduce the species.
Off Battersea Park, the Albert Bridge beyond.

226∧   227∨   228∨

227 A bale of hay at Tower Bridge. When one of London's bridges is under repair, hay is hung from the scaffolding as a warning to shipping. This custom is said to date back to Roman times. Hay was easier to find in horse transport days; there was a hay and straw market near here in Whitechapel High Street.
Tower Bridge, E1

228 A chimney on a bridge? One might be forgiven for thinking that a chimney on the parapet of Tower Bridge was a whimsical joke on the part of the architect. Actually there is a small guardroom built into the parapet and the chimney serves the fireplace of this room.

bomb site back to life. Fireworks and music were enjoyed again in the context of the river. The South Bank became a permanent centre for the arts, and now the National Theatre has joined the three concert halls, the art gallery and the film theatre already beside the river near Waterloo Bridge. Upstream at Battersea, not far from the site of Vauxhall pleasure gardens, is another riverside legacy of the Festival – the funfair.

Pageantry is returning to the Thames too. At the State funeral of Sir Winston Churchill the bier was carried on the Thames, past the cranes of Hays Wharf which dipped in a poignant salute. In 1976 a river procession was a feature of the Lord Mayor's Show and in 1977 the Queen's Silver Jubilee celebrations featured a royal pageant on the Thames.

The Thames has a fitting symbol for its clean and lively new image. This is the new London Bridge, officially opened in 1973. The new bridge was put up and the old one dismantled in progression, so that traffic across it never stopped. Strangely the pedestrian footways are wider on the downstream side than on the upstream. Statistics had shown that seven out of ten pedestrians crossed the old bridge on the downstream side. Old London Bridge, designed by John Rennie and originally opened in 1831, presides now over Lake Havasu in Arizona. When the first shipment of stones arrived at Long Beach docks in California, the bridge was classified by Customs as a "large antique."

Traces remain in London of the bridge that preceded Rennie's construction. The medieval London Bridge, surmounted by houses and shops, was regarded as one of the wonders of the world. It was built between 1176 and 1209, and its twenty stone piers survived the battering of the Thames currents until the nineteenth century. The great stone gate to the bridge was rebuilt in 1728, and the Coat of Arms of George II was affixed to it. When the gate was demolished in 1760 the Coat of Arms was sold to a stone mason in Newcomen Street in Southwark. There it can be seen still, serving as the inn sign for the King's Arms. Nearby, in Guys Hospital, is a stone alcove that dates from the widening of London Bridge in the 1760's.

The most extraordinary survival concerns a water-wheel that was erected in the northernmost arch of the medieval bridge in 1582. A Dutch engineer, named Pieter Morice devised the wheel, which used water power to pump up water from the river to supply the households of the City. He was granted a lease of the arch for five hundred years, for ten shillings a year. The waterworks were finally removed in 1822. But as Pieter Morice's heirs lost their revenue from the wheel, compensation had to be paid. Every year the Thames Water Authority still pays the sum of £3,750 to shareholders of the long-vanished waterworks, and will continue to do so until the five hundred years lease expires in AD 2082.

229 A Thames sailing barge, moored at St Katherine's Dock, near Tower Bridge. The annual sailing race for oyster smacks between Gravesend and London has recently been revived.

Swan Upping
230 The Royal Keeper of the Swans and his crew, about to set off up the Thames on the annual swan-upping voyage. In the course of a week they will row up river as far as Henley, catching and marking the young swans. The swan is regarded as a royal bird but the Queen shares the ownership of the Thames swans with two of the City Livery Companies, the Vintners' and the Dyers' who also provide swan-upping boats and crews. A young swan is marked on the beak, with the same mark that its mother has. The Vintners' swans have two nicks; the Dyers' swans have one nick; the Queen's swans are left unmarked.
Early July: The Temple Stairs, Victoria Embankment, WC2

231 Early monarchs of England gave chosen noblemen the privilege of owning swans. Each would nick the beaks of their birds with their own particular marks. A manuscript in the Museum of the Public Records Office, Chancery Lane, shows the wide choice of cuts that were inflicted upon the unfortunate birds.

232 St Paul's Cathedral in the palm of her hand, a statue known to watermen as "Little St Paul's on the Water."
On Vauxhall Bridge (South side)

229▽

230∧ 231∨ 232∨

Southwark's riverside

One of London's charms is the sudden change of mood between one street and the next, and even within the length of a single street. Nowhere are the changes of atmosphere more spectacular than in the Thameside borough of Southwark.

London Bridge station spills the visitor into Southwark with a tide of City workers, who surge across the bridge to their offices. In a dip, just below the hectic approaches to London Bridge rests the solid and tranquil form of Southwark Cathedral. Beyond it, almost overflowing into the cathedral precincts, is the bustling activity of the Borough Market, one of London's longest established fruit and vegetable markets. From the thirteenth century the market was held on London Bridge itself, and moved here in 1765. Leading off the market is a cobbled street, with the sinister name "Clink" marked upon its bollards. Clink Street bends between the towering black walls of the empty riverside warehouses. Suddenly a gap in this claustrophobic facade reveals the stone tracery of a fourteenth century rose window, an isolated fragment of the Great Hall of the Bishop of Winchester's palace. Further on, in Park Street, with the rumble of another main thoroughfare overhead, a bronze plaque declares that here stood Shakespeare's Globe Playhouse. Here a brewery now stands. Bankside in Elizabethan times was a pleasure centre for citizens from across the river. Bear-baiting and prostitution were banned within the City but flourished here. Bankside was known as Stew Bank from the rows of brothels that proclaimed their wares to the City on huge painted riverside signs.

There was only one bridge across the Thames between Roman times and 1749 and that was London Bridge. All roads to London from the south of England converged upon the bridgehead at Southwark. Hostelries for travellers were an early feature of Southwark and Geoffrey Chaucer despatched his pilgrims on their journey to Canterbury from one such inn, the Tabard; Talbot Yard marks the site. John Harvard owned an inn nearby called the Queen's Head; he sold it and the proceeds formed part of his gift to the American university that takes his name. The seventeenth-century George, off 71 Borough High Street, is London's last remaining coaching inn with galleries, which once formed a complete square around its courtyard; now only a precious fragment remains.

233 Derelict warehouses in Southwark. Fragments of the ancient town house of the Bishop of Winchester survive in the walls of this square.
Winchester Sq, Southwark, SE1

234 Just upstream of London Bridge, looking towards Southwark Cathedral.
Wharfside, EC4

<233

London dress

Hazlitt said that you can dress up in fantastic clothes or behave in a fantastic fashion in the street and not a soul will take any notice of you. Although Hazlitt died in 1830 his dictum still seems to hold good in London today, with only slight qualification. When a costume is worn with the dignity that comes of custom and habit it never seems ridiculous. But when a person feels uncomfortable and self-conscious in a uniform then he begins to look absurd and his costume becomes fancy dress. In the same way a ceremony or ritual remains convincing so long as its participants understand its history and are certain of its value. As soon as an event is re-enacted solely as a public spectacle it becomes, at best, theatre and, at worst, pantomime.

The purest origin of any form of dress is function. The heavy leather hat and boots of the Billingsgate fish porter are entirely functional, without so much as a nod towards fashion. Surprisingly the Bowler hat was conceived as functional headgear too. When a Norfolk landowner named Coke ordered the first Bowler hat from Lock's of St James's, he wanted a compact hard hat for his gamekeepers to wear. The Bowler gave all the protection that was needed but was not brushed off by low branches as was the top hat. Only later did the Bowler come to assume a different role, as the badge or uniform of a particular type of Londoner.

Some forms of dress originate not so much from function but to distinguish their wearers from everybody else. Military uniforms fall into this category. They are designed for instant recognition of friend or foe, officer or subordinate. Interestingly the officers of the Regiment of Guards, even when off duty and out of uniform, are recognized by their subordinates from their civilian form of dress. Visitors to the Horse Guards at Whitehall are puzzled when the sentries come smartly to attention for no apparent reason. But they have failed to notice what the sentry never misses. The gentleman walking past, with tightly furled umbrella and neat Bowler hat, is a Guards officer in civilian dress and the sentry must salute him.

When the First Guards of the British Army beat the French Grenadiers at Waterloo, they took over both the name and part of the uniform of their defeated enemy. The First Guards became the Grenadiers, and

235 A Chelsea Pensioner in summer uniform with a sergeant's stripes.

with the change of name came the grenade-thrower's bearskin hat. This "busby" also became ceremonial dress for the other regiments of Foot Guards in 1831.

Uniforms denote membership. And membership inevitably denotes exclusion of others. Badges and emblems, embroidered crests, club and school ties, are exclusive forms of dress that fellow members can recognize. The members of the City Companies are known collectively as the "Livery" by virtue of the livery costume that membership entitles them to wear. Likewise the servants of the Royal Family or of a nobleman are sometimes known as the "Livery" because they wear the uniforms that are exclusive to their household.

Formal civilian dress is worn relatively rarely now. Morning coats and top hats can be seen making their way to investitures and garden parties at Buckingham Palace, although Cabinet Ministers have been known to wear ordinary suits. Men's formal evening dress of white tie, winged collar and swallowtail coat is worn more commonly by waiters than by the diners that they serve; and by concert musicians rather than their audiences.

Some forms of dress are everyday costumes from the past that have become frozen at a particular stage in their development. The wig and knee breeches of a judge are examples of this phenomenon. If we could travel back to eighteenth century London we would be surprised to see how many judges there were in the streets, until we realised that wig and breeches were worn by most gentlemen of the period. Wigs went out of fashion partly as a result of William Pitt's tax on hair powder in 1793, but judges continued to wear them. Bishops too wore grey wigs well into the nineteenth century, and they still wear knee breeches today.

Some forms of dress are vestigial relics, like the appendix in the human body which once served a useful function but which has long ceased to do so. Barristers still have a pouch in their gowns. Barristers' fees were not recoverable in law and so their clients were by honour bound to slip their fees into this pouch.

There is a marked rejection of all kinds of formal dress among young people today, largely for egalitarian motives. But a glance at the crowds at a pop festival or a football match reveals how difficult it is to resist wearing a uniform that fellow travellers can instantly recognize.

236 A gold trimmed velvet coat, with silver badge, a lace neck-tie or "jabot," and white knee-breeches make the ceremonial uniform of the footman to the Aldermanic Sheriff of the City of London. The footman accompanies the Sheriff in his duties at the Central Criminal Court, the Old Bailey.

237 The Lord Chancellor's Tipstaff gets his name from the small metal-tipped rod that is his badge of office. The Tipstaff is an officer of the High Court of Justice. He executes the orders of the High Court and has powers to arrest offenders. He walks ahead of the Lord Chancellor on ceremonial occasions.

238 The head doorman at Lloyd's of London, the centre of world insurance. The red coat gives this gentleman a regal authority which is not, however, unique in London. The doorkeeper at the House of Lords wears a red tail-coat, by virtue of which he is known by the official title "Red Coat."

242 The Bargemaster of the Fishmongers' Company. The holder of this appointment is chosen from the most distinguished watermen to have won Doggett's coat and badge race. The Company no longer has a State Barge, but the Bargemaster acts as umpire at Doggett's race in a small motor boat.

243 A Waiter at Lloyds of London. Lloyds is now a vast insurance complex, but it started from modest beginnings, in the eighteenth-century coffee shop of Mr Edward Lloyd at 16 Lombard Street. The porters at Lloyds still wear waiters' livery in recognition of the firm's more modest origin.

244 A young campaigner of the Salvation Army. William Booth founded the movement in the East End of London in 1865, and it has since become established in eighty countries. The uniform is prim but not unflattering; the dainty bonnet with its maroon ribbon has become a symbol of real charity.

239 A beadle to one of the City's Aldermen. The beadle attends his Alderman at all ceremonial functions, and carries the mace belonging to that Alderman's particular ward. The City beadles are on duty at about ten occasions each year; most of them are retired men, some of whom come up from the country.

240 A Yeoman Warder at the Tower of London, in everyday dress, which has not changed since Tudor times. The Yeoman Warders' state dress, which is red trimmed with gold, is almost identical to that of a separate body of men, the Queen's Yeomen of the Guard, who are also known as beef-eaters (*boufetiers du roi*).

241 A fish porter at Billingsgate, wearing the traditional headgear. This particular hat is fifty-four years old and belonged to the wearer's father. It is made of thick leather, fixed with rivets, reinforced with wood and sealed with pitch. Porters' hats are heirlooms now as there is nobody left who can make them.

245 The Wine Porter of the Vintners' Company, serving as the official roadsweeper (see title page). He wears the wine porter's traditional smock, and carries the besom broom used by roadsweepers up to the turn of the century. For his top hat there is no obvious explanation – it just looks right.

246 A modern roadsweeper employed by the Westminster City Council. The Council's badge appears on the cap. The whole uniform, right down to the boots, is Council issue, but nevertheless each man manages to carry his clothes with an individual style which contradicts the official uniformity of dress.

247 The Sword Bearer of the Order of Bards, Ovates and Druids. The Druids' costume has not changed since the revival of interest in the sect in the 18th century. At that time the choice of clothes must surely have been influenced by the dress worn by Christian priests. The ancient Druids probably went naked.

248 A doorman at Claridges Hotel. Door-men are known as "linkmen," a term used in Elizabethan times for torchbearers. Now they serve as a link between the private interior of the hotel and the outside world. A linkman's livery must be splendid but not overblown to create the right balance of dignity and service.

249 Pink tailcoat, red waistcoat and gold-trimmed top hat are worn by doormen of the Bank of England. This flash of gold is a reminder that this great institution stores and controls Britain's gold reserve. Top hats have another association with the Bank: people visiting the Governor should wear one.

250 The Pearly King of Lambeth, Ted Marriott, who is also Chairman of the Pearly Kings and Queens Association. There are about 35,000 pearly buttons on his costume. The trousers were handed down by his father and are almost fifty years old. Some pearly king's suits weigh over sixty pounds.

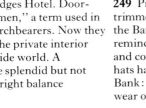

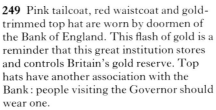

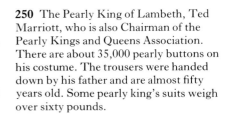

254 Doggett's Coat and Badge. The prize in the world's longest surviving rowing race is the right to wear this uniform. In 1715 a comedian called Thomas Doggett set up the race to commemorate the Accession to the throne of George I. The silver badge bears an image of the white horse of Hanover.

255 A trooper of the Blues and Royals. The mounted squadrons of this regiment and of the Life Guards form the Household Cavalry. This provides the Sovereign's Escort on state occasions and mounts the Queen's Life Guard daily. Members of the Blues and Royals also serve as tank and armoured car personnel.

256 The Lady of Autumn is a non-Druid who is invited to attend the Druid ceremonies at the autumn equinox. In country districts she would be the wife of the farmer on whose land the celebrations were held. Turned inside out, her cloak serves as the green costume for the celebration of the spring equinox.

251 The uniform of a Pensioner at the Royal Hospital, Chelsea, is based upon the British Army uniform at the time of the Duke of Marlborough's campaigns. The scarlet coat is the Pensioners' summer plumage, which appears for the first time at the Founder's Day Parade in May. The winter uniform is blue.

252 The Swan Herd of the Vintners' Company. This gentleman has the pleasant job of looking after the swans on the Thames, and this is his ceremonial uniform and badge of office. The Vintners' Company share ownership of the Thames swans with Her Majesty the Queen and the Dyers' Company.

253 The Swan Herd of the Vintners' Company, in his working blazer. He is just about to embark on the swan-upping voyage from the Temple to Henley (see page 109). The Vintners' young swans will be marked with two nicks in their bills, which explains the corrupted origin of the pub name "Swan with two Necks."

257 A dismounted trooper of the Life Guards on duty at the Horse Guards in Whitehall. The Life Guards are the senior regiment of the British Army, and were formed from King Charles II's personal bodyguard. Off duty Guards officers have their own uniform, a smartly rolled umbrella and a bowler hat.

258 The King's Troop of the Royal Horse Artillery. This regiment parades in Hyde Park on Royal Anniversaries to give the twenty-one gun salute. The cross-bands on the chest of the uniform are said to be based upon the pattern of the ribcage of a skeleton, and were intended to instil terror in the enemy in battle.

259 This sentry at St James's Palace is a member of the Coldstream Guards. The five Guards Regiments can be distinguished by the arrangements of buttons on their tunics. The Grenadier Guards have an even row of buttons, the Coldstream have them in twos, the Scots in threes, the Irish fours and the Welsh fives.

A taste of London

The unfortunate Marie Antoinette is best remembered for her careless remark about the Parisians' diet. "Let them eat cake!" was bait to a starving populace on the brink of revolution. London has a story of an equally insensitive remark which had a milder, though no less effective, sequel. Lord Claud Hamilton, who became Chairman of the Great Eastern Railway at Liverpool Street in 1893 said that the average railwayman ought to be able to do a good day's work on the nourishment to be found in a single bloater: this is a London speciality, a particular kind of smoked herring. At a mass meeting of his employees a little later, his Lordship was bothered by the distinctly unsavoury atmosphere of the hall. Each man had brought with him one ripe and malodorous bloater. Lord Hamilton did not lose his head, but he did not comment on the Londoners' diet again.

A Londoner enjoys his fish. From Whitechapel to Woolwich the taste is for eels and shellfish. The East Ender likes to stand at a street stall and eat cold eel in jelly, or a dish of whelks or cockles with a sprinkling of vinegar. He buys his eels alive for home consumption and waits while they are beheaded on a marble slab. Gentlemen of the City like to sit down at white tablecloths to consume shellfish and fish pie at Sweetings oyster establishment in Queen Victoria Street. In the West End, restaurants like Wiltons, Sheekeys, Overtons, Wheelers and Bentleys have built great reputations on their cuisine of fine fish, cooked simply but well.

Eels are not much liked outside London but these fish are trapped for the London market mainly in Norfolk. Cockles are dug from the Essex sands. Prawns and winkles come from further afield. Eating habits do not change a great deal as they are passed down from one generation to another and it seems possible that the Londoner's fish habit is an inheritance from his ancestors. Salmon have not been caught in the Thames since 1833 but before that time there was such a wealth of fish in the river that apprentices used to complain about their unvaried diet of salmon. Shellfish could be dug from the mudflats at low tide and eels used to wriggle up every little tributary and drain. So fish would have been the most easily obtainable food in the City. It was one commodity that poor people could get for nothing. So a palate for cockles and eels might even have been a requirement for survival through hard times.

In Essex Street, Islington, in Tower Bridge Road and in Peckham High Street among other places, one may catch a whiff of a characteristic aroma from the back of fish shops, where eels, haddock and trout are smoked with gently smouldering oak shavings. Another salubrious smell fills the air in districts surrounding the main London breweries at Bankside, Finsbury, Wandsworth and Whitechapel. Most of the 7,000-odd London pubs are owned by one or other of the London breweries and yet a large proportion retain their own distinct character, mysteriously compounded from both the surroundings and the customers themselves.

Some pubs have honky-tonk pianos and go in for singing on Saturday nights; others give sophisticated jazz concerts or lunchtime theatre shows. Pubs in the East End may lay on strip-tease during the week and prawns and winkles on Sundays. A unique form of London skittles is played at the Duke's Head in Putney and at the Freemason's Arms in Hampstead – where Pell-Mell can also be seen in the garden in summer. The Pell-Mell player holds a heavy stone ball in a ring at the end of a stick. He jerks the stick in an attempt to toss the ball through a hoop set into the ground.

Charles II used to play Real (Royal) Tennis at Orange Street, off the Haymarket, and the name of the pub there, the Hand and Racquet, recalls the connection. Some of the most familiar pub names have royal origins. Many derive from royal badges or emblems, like the White Hart (Richard II), the Rising Sun (Edward III), the Red Lion (John of Gaunt, Duke of Lancaster), the Greyhound (Henry VII). The Rose and Crown marks the marriage of Elizabeth, the White Rose of York, with the King, Henry of Lancaster, and thus symbolizes the end of the Wars of the Roses. Pub names were passed down and a name of ancient origin does not necessarily mean that the pub itself is old.

The Angel, Islington, The Royal Oak near Paddington, and the Swiss Cottage near Hampstead demonstrate the significance of pubs in the geography of London. They were such landmarks that whole districts were named after them.

260 Engraved glass at a nineteenth century pub. Victorian pubs gave a wider choice than modern ones, with public, saloon, private and ladies' bars. The "Bottle and Jug" counter was for off-licence sales. Here one could buy liquor by the bottle, and bring jugs to be filled with beer.
Bunch of Grapes, Brompton Rd, Knightsbridge, SW3

261 An unusual feature in a Victorian pub, a "snob-screen," of decorative frosted glass. This screen divides a ladies' bar from the serving counter, and was intended to give women privacy from the rest of the pub.
The Prince Alfred, Formosa St, Maida Vale, W9

Pub games: London skittles
262, 263 The form of skittles played in London pubs is more skilful than country skittles. Instead of a ball, a heavy hardwood disc, a "cheese," is hurled at the nine pins. The combination of pins that are left standing have colourful names that include: "Waterloo," "Novice," "London Bridge," "Gates of Hell" and "Cocked Hat."
The Freemason's Arms, Downshire Hill, Hampstead, NW3

261∧

262∧

263∨

Pub Fronts

264 An unsuitably slim building for the fat Friar above the door. Inside, this Edwardian pub is decorated with more images of friars, in a strange *art nouveau* style.
The Blackfriar, Queen Victoria St, EC4

265 *The Flask, Highgate West Hill, N6*

266 *The Red Lion, Duke of York St, St James's, SW1*

267 *The Ladbroke Arms, Ladbroke Rd, W11*

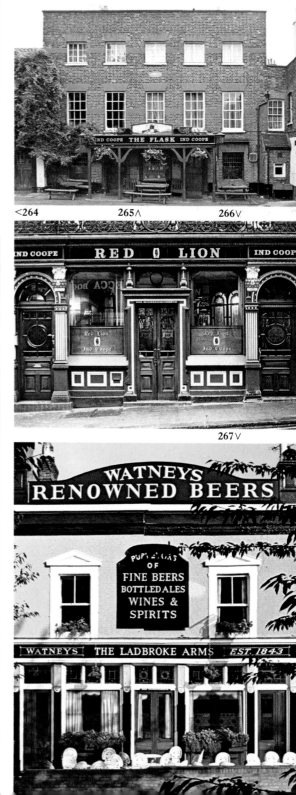

<264 265∧ 266∨

267∨

Windward of London Bridge the air has been enriched with the sharp tang of fish for almost a thousand years. Billingsgate wharf was one of the first landing stages in regular use on the Thames and there was a wholesale fish market here centuries before the present one was built in 1877. Now some 55,000 tons of fish pass through the market every year.

Fish wives are proverbial for bad language and "billingsgate" appears in dictionaries as an adjective for abusive language. Present-day fish porters do not deserve this notoriety any more than other men doing heavy work at high speed.

A legendary cafe near Billingsgate Market is said to have served soup from a copper cauldron that was constantly replenished and never allowed to run dry. One day it was inadvertently emptied and among the dregs at the bottom was revealed a well-cooked but perfectly intact fish porter's hat. These hats are reputed to have been based upon the design of the protective helmets of wood and leather that were worn by the English archers at Agincourt.

From the twelfth century Smithfield was a "smooth field" where open air livestock markets were held. The bloody associations of the district are not restricted to the slaughter of livestock. Here public executions also took place. Between 1554 and 1558, in the reign of the Catholic Queen Mary I, some 200 protestants were burnt at the stake at Smithfield.

Smithfield today is Britain's largest meat market. There are over 15 miles of meat hooks within the covered halls. Some 3,000 people are employed in the markets and the average annual turnover is around 300,000 tons of meat. This represents about 725,000 head of beef, some 3 million lambs, 900,000 pigs and 21 million head of poultry. This astonishing quantity of merchandise changes hands within a quarter of a mile of St Paul's Cathedral at the heart of London. All the action at Smithfield, as in other wholesale markets, takes place in the early hours of the morning: when the City comes to work at about 9 am, the place is clean, tidy and almost empty as if nothing had happened. The market pubs are open from 6.30 am and porters can drink there after work until they close at 9.30 am.

The turnover of London's food markets is such that almost all merchandise is sold on the day that it comes in. London's huge appetite means that it enjoys its food fresh.

268 Menu for a working man. *Don's cafe, 674 Holloway Rd, N1*

269 The chop house is a London eating place, as opposed to the steak house which is an American import. Note the window signs: "London's noted cup of tea" and "Progressive working class caterer." *Quality Chop House, Farringdon Rd, Mount Pleasant, EC1*

270 Cheese in St James's. *Paxton & Whitfield, Jermyn St, SW1*

271 Vegetable stall. *Berwick St Market, Soho, W1*

272 Wholesale meat market. *Smithfield, EC1*

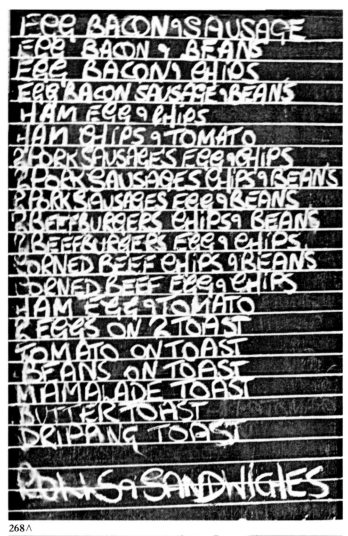

268∧

270∧

271∨

London's taste for fish

273 Live eels for sale. This East End eel purveyor keeps three tons of live eels in tanks at the back of the shop.
F. Cooke, Kingsland High St, E8

274 Wholesale fish market.
Billingsgate EC3

275 East End shellfish stall.
Tubby Isaacs, Goulston St, Aldgate, E1

276 The best shellfish display in East London, Wally Herbert's Sunday morning stall in Bethnal Green. Everything is sold by afternoon.
Brick Lane, Bethnal Green, E2

277 "If it swims, we sell it:" the words of Harrods' fish buyer, Jim Sneath are an echo of the firm's telegraphic address: *Everything London*. By 5.00 am Mr Sneath is down at Billingsgate market in his gum boots, up to his elbows in herrings and trading in language that the fish porters understand. He arranges this display before 9.00 am when the shop opens. By then he has donned his morning coat and is ready to receive his customers with the civility that is the mark of the best London stores.
The Food Hall, Harrods, Knightsbridge, SW1

273∧

274∧

275∨

276∨

Index

Subjects illustrated and those discussed in the captions are indexed by illustration numbers in bold. The main text is indexed by page numbers.

287 Westminster Abbey, seen from Millbank, with a sculpture by Henry Moore in the foreground. The Abbey is largely gothic, of the thirteenth century, but the twin towers are eighteenth-century additions by Nicholas Hawksmoor.

Bibliography

Conrad Bailey, *Famous London Graves*, Harrap 1975
Margaret Baker, *Discovering London: Statues and Monuments*, Shire Publications 1968
Felix Barker & Peter Jackson, *London, 2000 years of a City*, Cassell 1974
W. G. Bell, *Unknown London & More about Unknown London*, Bodley Head 1921
Pearl Binder, *The Pearlies*, Jupiter Books 1975
Charles Booth, *Life and Labour of London*, Williams & Norgate 1889
Margaret Brentnall, *The Old Customs and Ceremonies of London*, Batsford 1975
G. Cobb, *The Old Churches of London*, Batsford 1948 (Revised 1977)
Len Deighton, *London Dossier*, Penguin 1966
Blake Ehrlich, *London on the Thames*, Cassell 1968
Richard Fitter, *London's Natural History*, Collins 1945
Margaret Gascoigne, *Discovering English Customs and Traditions*, Shire Publications 1969
Mark Girouard, *Victorian Pubs*, Studio Vista 1976
Walter H. Godfrey, *A History of Architecture in and around London*, Phoenix House (Revised 1962)

Greater London Council, *Blue Plaque Guide*, G.L.C. 1976
Philip Howard, *London's River*, Hamish Hamilton 1975
Peter Jackson, *London is stranger than fiction*, Associated Newspapers 1951
Peter Jackson, *The London Explorer*, Associated Newspapers 1953
Peter Jackson, *London Bridge*, Cassell 1971
Eric de Mare, *London's Riverside*, Max Reinhardt 1958
Roger Milton, *The English Ceremonial Book*, David & Charles 1972
Ian Nairn, *Nairn's London*, Penguin 1966
Nikolaus Pevsner, *The Buildings of England; London vols 1 & 2*, Penguin (Revised 1973)
David Piper, *The Companion Guide to London*, Fontana Collins 1970
Ernest Pooley, *The Guilds of the City of London*, Collins 1945
V. S. Pritchett, *London Perceived* (photographs by Evelyn Hofer), Chatto & Windus 1962
John Pudney, *London Docks*, Thames & Hudson 1975
John Summerson, *Georgian London*, Penguin 1962
Geoffrey Trease, *London, a Concise History*, Thames & Hudson 1975
H. B. Wheatley, *London Past & Present*, John Murray 1891